SCHOOL POWER

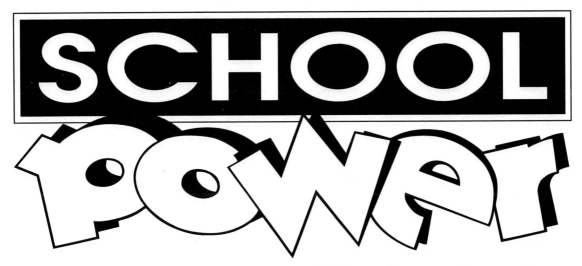

Strategies for Succeeding in School

Jeanne Shay Schumm, ph.d.
and Marguerite Radencich, ph.d.

free spirit
PUBLISHING
Works
for kids

W9-BDF-152

dedication

To our parents, Vera and Jim, Felicita and Eugenio, and to Jamie

acknowledgments

Because SCHOOL POWER is a book for middle school students, we decided to involve some students your age in the development of our book. Each of our Advisory Board members provided GREAT suggestions! We want to thank each one for their time and for their comments.

Diana Lia Barrios, St. Louis, Missouri

Cayson Ellsworth, Port St. Lucie, Florida

Marc Flash, Ft. Lauderdale, Florida

Sean Guest, Miami, Florida

Michelle Lippett, St. Louis, Missouri

Adam Schumm, Richmond, Virginia

Julie Schumm, Stuart, Florida

Nicholas Schumm, Pensacola, Florida

Sarah Shay, Port St. Lucie, Florida

Colby Thomas, Sherborn, Massachusetts

Editor
Pamela Espeland

Art Direction
MacLean & Tuminelly

Photographer
Teresa Van Hatten

Cover illustration
Suzanne Brill

Text illustration
Barb Spies

Index
Eileen Quam and Theresa Wolner

Free Spirit Publishing Inc.
400 First Avenue North, Suite 616
Minneapolis, MN 55401
(612) 338-2068

Publisher and President
Judy Galbraith

Editorial Assistant
M. Elizabeth Salzmann

Art Department
Suzanne Brill, Lucy Grantz, Chris Long, Mike Tuminelly, Nancy Tuminelly, Lisa Wagner

Production
Lisa Duncan

Copyright © 1992 by Jeanne Shay Schumm and Marguerite C. Radencich

All rights reserved. Unless otherwise noted, no part of this book may be reproduced in any form, except for brief reviews, without written permission of the publisher

Library of Congress Cataloging-in-Publication Data

Schumm, Jeanne Shay, 1947–
    School power : strategies for succeeding in school / by Jeanne Shay Schumm and Marguerite C. Radencich ; edited by Pamela Espeland.
        p. cm.
    Includes bibliographical references and index.
    Summary: Discusses better ways of organizing time, keeping track of assignments, listening, taking notes, participating in class, reading, writing, and preparing for tests.
    ISBN 0-915793-42-3 :
    1. Study, Method of—Juvenile literature. [1. Study, Method of.]
I. Radencich, Marguerite, 1952– .
II. Espeland, Pamela, 1951– . III. Title.
LB1601.S37 1992
371.3'02812—dc20
                        92-10907
                        CIP
                        AC

10 9 8 7

Printed in the United States of America

If you're busy adjusting to life in middle school/junior high—getting used to changing classes, coping with different teachers' styles and rules, following a schedule that can be confusing—SCHOOL POWER is for you. Even if you're not in middle school, it will help you make it through whatever grade you're in.

This isn't an ordinary school book or textbook. It's a how-to guide for just about everything you need to know to succeed in school. Would you like to be able to read faster? See pages 38–39. Would you like to take better notes in class? Check out pages 17–24. Do you hate to write? Turn to page 48. Do you lose track of long-range projects? Find help on page 12. Is it hard for you to talk to your teachers? See page 11 for suggestions. Scan the Contents and the Index; they'll point you toward the tips, techniques, and strategies you need.

Keep this guide handy every day—on your desk, with your textbooks, anywhere in easy reach. Stick it in your backpack along with your daily homework assignments. Write notes in it, highlight important points, mark key pages with colored clips or post-its. Turn to it whenever you need to review an important procedure or tackle a problem. Use it regularly and you'll find school getting easier, more manageable—maybe even more fun.

Thanks to the Clara Barton Open School, Minneapolis, MN and Earl Brown Elementary School, Brooklyn Center, MN and their teachers for allowing us to photograph them for SCHOOL POWER!

• •

Some of the information in "Listen and Take Notes" on pages 15-24 originally appeared in Schumm, J.S., & Lopate, K., "An 8-step instructional plan for teaching notetaking skills to middle school students." *Florida Reading Quarterly* (1989).

The Cornell note-taking system on pages 20-21 was originally described in Pauk, W., *How to Study in College.* 2nd. ed. Boston: Houghton Mifflin, 1974.

The FLIP strategy on pages 33-34 is adapted from Schumm, J.S., & Mangrum, C.T. (1991), "FLIP: A framework for content area reading." *Journal of Reading,* 35 (2), 120-124.

The All About Whales Semantic Mapping example on page 37 is from Kuchinskas, Gloria, and Radencich, Marguerite C., *The Semantic Mapper.* Gainesville, FL: Teacher Support Software, 1986. Reprinted with permission of Teacher Support Software.

Marc's First Draft, Revisions, Edits, and Final Draft on pages 53, 55, 57, and 58 are used with permission of Renee Flash.

The A-OK strategy on pages 54-58 is adapted with permission from "A-OK: A Reading for Revision Strategy" by Jeanne Shay Schumm in *Reading: Exploration and Discovery,* Vol. 10, No. 1, Fall, 1987.

The PORPE strategy on pages 76-77 was originally described in Simpson, M.L., "PORPE: A writing strategy for studying and learning in the content areas." *Journal of Reading,* 29 (1974): 407-414.

The STAR strategy on page 77 was originally described in Radencich, Marguerite C., "S.T.A.R., a strategy for taking timed tests." *Forum for Reading,* 17 (Fall/Winter 1985): 29-34. Reprinted with permission of Dr. Rona Flippo.

Spelling Demons and Spelling Demons II on pages 113 and 114 are from Fry, E.B., Polk, J.K., and Fountoukidis, D., *The Reading Teacher's Book of Lists.* Englewood Cliffs, NJ: Prentice Hall, 1984. Reprinted with permission of Edward Fry, Ph.D.

Contents

tools for school success.....83

GET YOUR ACT together

oRgaNize YouR Life

When you were in the lower grades, organizing your life was easy. Why? Because you didn't have to do it! Your parents probably organized your time at home. Your teacher structured your time at school. Now it's up to **you** to keep track of your tasks and activities.

Organizing your life takes time and effort, but it's worth it because...

...organizing your life can improve your success in school, ...organizing your life can help you avoid last-minute rushes and cram-a-thons, and ...organizing your life can help you persuade teachers and parents that you're becoming more mature and independent. You'll earn more privileges and freedom.

1

Set Up a Home Study Center

Some people can study in the middle of blaring TVs and radios, ringing phones, battling brothers and sisters, barking family dogs, and busy parents. Maybe you're one of these people, but probably you're not. You'll study better if you follow these guidelines.

LOCATION

Try to find a quiet place that's free from distractions (no phone, no Nintendo). Choose a place where you don't do other things. For example, if you study on your bed, you'll start thinking about falling asleep, and pretty soon...zzzzzz....

LIGHTING

Some students like it bright, while others choose softer lighting. Natural light is best for you, but whatever light you use, make sure there's enough to read and work by without straining your eyes. **A lamp should shed light over your shoulder. It should not be aimed straight at the printed page.**

SEATING

It's okay to slump into a beanbag chair to read a story. But when you really want to concentrate, try a straight-backed chair at a table or desk.

NOISE

Try to pick a place away from the center of activity. Post a personalized DO NOT DISTURB sign to let others know you're working.

SUPPLIES

Many students waste valuable time searching for study supplies. You can be more efficient. Keep these things handy on your desk, in a shoebox, or in a plastic shopping bag.

- ✔ pencils
- ✔ pens
- ✔ erasers
- ✔ markers
- ✔ writing paper
- ✔ tape
- ✔ a hole punch
- ✔ a pencil sharpener
- ✔ glue or paste
- ✔ a ruler
- ✔ a stapler
- ✔ colored pencils
- ✔ paper clips
- ✔ index cards
- ✔ a calculator
- ✔ (anything else?)

Stocking a study center can get expensive. If there's something you need and don't have, talk it over with your teachers. They may have extra supplies on hand.

REFERENCES

Build a small personal library, with at least a dictionary and a thesaurus. Also useful: a one-volume desk encyclopedia, a set of encyclopedias (if your family has one), or access to an on-line encyclopedia through a computer service like Prodigy.

Add an almanac, an atlas, and other references as you need them. Example: if you're taking Spanish, you'll probably want a Spanish-English dictionary.

BULLETIN BOARD

Use it to post calendars, important notices, and directions for special projects. Leave room for postcards, pictures, and cartoons. Your study center doesn't have to be boring.

MICHELLE'S tip for students ON THE go

Michelle is a competitive swimmer who practices 20 hours a week and goes to swim meets on a regular basis. To keep up with her school work, she keeps a "study kit" in the family car. This kit includes many of the items on our Supplies list—plus a lapboard. This allows Michelle to study in the car on her way to practices, and at meets while waiting for her event.

How to Organize Your Learning Environment

KEEP IT SIMPLE

The more you have to keep track of, the more likely you are to lose something. Before you add another notebook, bookbag, or backpack, ask, "Do I REALLY need this?"

Prevent learning environment pollution. Backpacks, bookbags, notebooks, and lockers can become catchalls, garbage dumps, and toxic waste sites.

BACKPACKS, BOOKBAGS, AND NOTEBOOKS

If you throw things in your backpack, bookbag, or notebook all day long, start your after-school studies with a five-minute cleanup.

Each night before you go to bed, make sure you have everything you need for the next day, stored in your backpack or bookbag and ready to go. Leave it all in a convenient, regular place for pickup in the morning.

LOCKERS

Trash those old papers, bologna sandwiches, and smelly P.E. sneakers. Post a copy of your daily schedule inside the door. See page 6 for tips on making a daily schedule.

How to Organize Your Time

POCKET CALENDARS AND ASSIGNMENT NOTEBOOKS

A pocket calendar or assignment notebook is a *must*. Carry it with you to all your classes. Use it to record assignment due dates, appointments (doctor, dentist, etc.), birthdays, special events, and vacations. About once every month, check your calendar against your family's schedule so you can record upcoming events and avoid conflicts.

➡ You don't need to buy an expensive calendar. Businesses often give away free pocket calendars for advertising purposes.

➡ Many middle school students like to use teacher planning calendars, available in school and office supply stores. Some of these come three-hole-punched to go in a looseleaf notebook.

➡ You can also find special student calendars with "to do" lists and pages for recording assignments.

Two companies that sell student calendars are:

Day-Timers, Inc.
One Day-Timer Plaza
Allentown, PA 18195-1551
215-395-5884

Franklin International Institute
2200 West Parkway Boulevard
Salt Lake City, UT 84119
801-975-1776

Call or write for their free catalogs.

	Monday	Tuesday	Wednesday	Thursday	Friday	Saturday	Sunday
8:00	Math	Math	Math	Math	Math		
9:00	Science	Art	Science	Art	Science		
10:00	Vocabulary/Reading	Vocabulary/Reading	Vocabulary/Reading	Vocabulary/Reading	Vocabulary/Reading	Scout	
11:00	Lunch	Lunch	Lunch	Lunch	Lunch		
12:00	Social Studies	Music	Social Studies	Music	Social Studies	Lunch	
1:00	Library Skills	Spanish	Library Skills	Spanish	Library Skills	Basketball Ga...	
2:00	P.E.	P.E.	P.E.	P.E.	P.E.		
3:00	Basketball Practice	Car Pool SNACK!	Basketball Practice	Car Pool SNACK!	Car Pool SNACK!		
4:00		Home-work		Home-work	FREE Time!	F...	
5:00	Car Pool / Home-work	FREE Time!	Car Pool / Home-work	FREE Time!			
6:00	Dinner	Dinner	Dinner	Dinner	Dinner		
7:00	Home-work	Home-work	Home-work	Home-work	Play practice		
8:00	Homework or TV	Homework or TV	Homework or TV	Homework or TV			
9:00	TV/Shower	TV/Shower	TV/Shower	TV/Shower			
10:00	Bed	Bed	Bed	Bed	Bed		

Nick's Schedule

Nick is in eighth grade. He enjoys sports and is on his school's basketball team. He is also an actor in community theater. Recently, he starred in a production of *Oliver*. Nick has a busy schedule, but he still manages to keep up with his homework AND have some free time. Here's how he does it.

WALL CALENDARS

Some students like to get the big picture by posting a wall calendar in their home study center or locker. They use it to jot down major events and deadlines.

Life is more complicated if you keep two calendars. But if a wall calendar works for you, use one.

DAILY SCHEDULES

Keeping track of your daily schedule is easy when you use a time management chart. Page 85 has a blank chart you can copy and use.

1. Start by writing in all of your regularly scheduled activities (classes, band practice, soccer practice, piano lessons).
2. Next, block out your homework time (math, reading, study time for tests).
3. Add your daily living activities (meals, sleep, chores).
4. Chart your personal time (TV, recreation, relaxation, friends).

Make copies of your time management chart for your notebook, your locker at school (if you have a locker), and your bulletin board at home. Revise your chart whenever there's a change in your regularly scheduled activities.

time management tips

Set priorities

If you have lots to do, make a list of everything, then rank each task in A-B-C order. Do the A task first, the B task second, and so on down through your list. You'll worry less and get more accomplished.

Find and use little chunks of time

Waiting for the bus, in between classes, just before your favorite TV show...these are all little chunks of time you can put to good use. Choose something small, get it done, and get it out of the way.

Plan some time just for fun

Recreational time helps keep you mentally and physically healthy. But get your work done first. Free time feels freer when you don't have unfinished business.

Don't over-schedule yourself

Some people overeat; others over-schedule themselves. If you have too much to do, you need to go on a schedule diet. Review your activities. Which ones can you live without?

Don't procrastinate

Most people procrastinate for a reason. Maybe the task they're facing is too hard. Maybe it's too stressful. Whatever the cause, procrastination can become a bad habit. The best cure is simply to dig in and do the job. If you really, truly can't get started, talk it over with a friend, a teacher, or another trusted adult.

Be flexible

Things change. Your schedule isn't carved in stone. Give yourself room to adapt to new circumstances and take advantage of new opportunities.

Plan time to get organized

Getting organized takes getting used to. Plan a few minutes each day to work on your schedules and clean up your learning environment. Think about what you need to do and how you're going to do it. You'll save hours of time you might have wasted.

cathy's tip for early-morning studying

Cathy likes to get up early in the morning to study and do final reviews for tests. She knows that this doesn't work for everyone, but she feels her best in the morning hours—fresh and alert. Cathy has recognized that she's a morning person. She organizes her time around that fact.

How to Keep Track of Daily Assignments

Some teachers write assignments on the board. Some give handouts that list the assignments for a week or a month. Some record assignments on an electronic telephone service, and students can dial in to get the message.

But other teachers just call out assignments at the end of class, and you can't hear because the bell is ringing and other kids are packing up their books and your friends are reminding you about basketball practice and someone knocked your notebooks on the floor....

No matter what, **you are responsible for knowing about and completing your assignments**. Don't leave class until you understand an assignment, even if it means staying after for a few minutes. Write down **all** assignments. Don't count on your memory.

"TO DO" LISTS

A "to do" list is a perfect place to record assignments. Write down directions as well as due dates.

ASSIGNMENT SHEETS

Some teachers provide assignment sheets. If yours don't, page 87 has one you can copy and use.

Use **one** assignment sheet for **all** of your classes. Slip it into the notebook you carry all the time. At the end of the day, use it like a shopping list to decide what you need to take home from your locker.

What good does Homework do?

Most teachers don't give homework just to make your life miserable. Homework can be good for you because...

...it encourages you to practice skills you have not fully learned yet,

...it gives you opportunities to review skills you might forget,

...it enriches your store of general knowledge, adding to what you already know and helping you to learn new things,

...it teaches you responsibility, and

...it allows for tasks that are too time-consuming to finish during regular school hours.

13 Terrible Excuses for Not Turning in Your Homework on Time

1 "I left it in my pocket and my mom put my jeans in the wash." **2** "I left it on the bus (on my bed, in my locker....)" **3** "The dog (cat, rat, computer) ate it." **4** "I didn't do it because I had soccer practice." **5** "I didn't do it because I left my books at school." **6** "I didn't do it because my mom (dad, sister, brother, aunt, grandmother) forgot to remind me." **7** "I didn't do it because I had to finish an assignment for another class." **8** "You didn't tell us to do it." **9** "I didn't hear you tell us to do it." **10** "I wasn't listening." **11** "It was due today?" **12** (Silence) **13** "What homework?"

How to Handle Homework Problems

•••••••••••••••••••••

problem •••••• "I have a lot of other things to do, so I don't have time for homework."

solution ••••► Homework is not an option. Eliminate some of your other activities.

problem •••••• "I let my homework go until the last minute."

solution ••••► Use assignment sheets. See page 8.

problem •••••• "I don't pay attention to how important homework is for my grade. Then it's too late."

solution ••••► Listen to your teachers when they tell you what counts in their classes. Most will base at least part of your grade on your homework.

problem •••••• "I forget to take my books home, or I forget to bring my homework to class."

solution ••••► See page 4 for tips on how to keep your materials organized in your locker and at home.

problem •••••• "I forget the instructions. Sometimes I don't understand them in the first place."

solution ••••► Write down all assignments and directions. If there's something you don't understand, ask the teacher or a friend to explain.

problem •••••• "I spend a lot of time on homework, but I still can't get it all done."

solution ••••► Are distractions keeping you from working (TV, phone calls, noise, interruptions)? If distractions aren't the problem, talk to your teachers. See if they have any suggestions.

problem •••••• "All of my teachers assign homework on the same day. Then they give tests on the same day. I can't keep up!"

solution ••••► Use assignment sheets to organize the assignments you know about in advance. Ask your teachers if they can give you longer lead times on some assignments. If your work still piles up, talk to your teachers. See if they're willing to compare their schedules and give assignments and tests on different days. If this doesn't work, take your problem to the student council or the school counselor.

What to Do If You Get Behind

Everyone gets behind in their homework sometimes. This can happen for a lot of reasons. People get sick, overschedule themselves, have personal problems, get disorganized—but mainly, people aren't perfect.

The key to getting out of the hole is not to fall too far in. As soon as you feel yourself slipping, do something! Use assignment sheets to organize your work. Update your pocket calendar or assignment notebook. Stick to your study schedule, and add time for make-up work.

If you still can't catch up, make an appointment to talk to your teachers. Consider inviting your parents, too. You'll probably surprise the socks off of everybody. But if you take the initiative, the grown-ups will know that you're serious about straightening out the mess you're in.

tips for talking to teachers

1 Think about what you want to say BEFORE you go into your meeting. Make notes and bring them along.

2 Choose your words carefully. Instead of saying, "I'm behind because YOU give too much homework," you might say, "I'm behind on my school work, and I want to catch up. Do you have any suggestions?"

3 Don't expect the teacher to have all the answers. Come prepared with your own ideas.

4 Be polite and respectful. Remember that the purpose of your meeting is conversation, not confrontation.

5 Focus on what you need, not on what you think the teacher is doing wrong. The more the teacher learns about you, the more he or she can help. The more defensive the teacher feels, the less he or she will want to help.

6 Don't forget to listen.

7 Bring your sense of humor. Not the joke-telling kind, but the kind that lets you laugh at yourself and your own mistakes.

8 If your meeting is a flop, get help from another adult. Talk to the school counselor or another teacher you know and trust. Pick someone you think is likely to want to help you. Then try again.

"When in doubt, tell the truth."
—Mark Twain

How to Keep Track of Long-Range Assignments

Art Fair, Science Fair, term papers, social studies displays....Special projects can be nightmares! They can also lead to last-minute panics and desperate acts, such as trying to write a 20-page research paper in a single night.

There's a guaranteed way to avoid the hassle and actually enjoy your long-range assignments. It's called P-L-A-N-N-I-N-G.

As soon as you hear about a long-range assignment, make a project plan. Follow this checklist, or copy and use the form on pages 89–90.

✔ **Decide on a project theme.**

✔ **Have the theme approved by your teacher.**

✔ **Make a list of things you need to do to complete your project. Rank them in the order they need to be done.**

✔ **Decide if you'll need help from your parents or other adults. Ask if and when they can help you. Be clear about what you want them to do.**

✔ **Set deadlines for finishing each part of your project. Write the dates in your assignment notebook or calendar.**

✔ **Make a list of materials you'll need. Estimate how much they will cost.**

✔ **Send away for resource materials.**

✔ **Contact community resources.**

✔ **Visit the library.**

✔ **Complete your project on schedule.**

cayson's tip for Long-range projects

Cayson's specialty is science fair projects. He has won awards for his research in sixth and seventh grades. Cayson's secret is to think of an idea early—even before the science fair project is assigned. That way, he can find a topic he is really interested in, begin gathering materials, and generally get a head start.

Plan to Succeed

Successful people don't become successful by accident or luck. They plan to succeed. They set goals and work to achieve them. They recognize problems that may get in their way, and come up with solutions.

You can plan to succeed. On pages 91–92, there's a goal-setting chart you can copy and use. Fill one out today. In two to four weeks, look back at your chart. Have your goals changed? Have you solved some of your problems? Have you had other successes? Add these to the Update section. Then fill out a new goal-setting chart.

Keep doing this throughout the school year—every month or so. At the end of the year, you'll have a record of your goals and successes.

p.s. It's nice to begin this goal-setting process at the start of a new school year. But you can do it anytime and get results.

the Checkpoint System: SIX STEPS to success

Before takeoff, an airplane pilot goes through a series of checkpoints to make sure that everything is ready for a safe journey. These six checkpoints will help you succeed at school.

✔ AT HOME

Before you leave the house, check to make sure you have everything you need for the day (backpack, bookbag, supplies, books, lunch, homework, signed notes, special projects, pocket calendar or assignment notebook, good mood...).

✔ AT YOUR LOCKER

Before going to class, stop at your locker (if you have one) and check to see that you have everything you need.

✔ IN CLASS

Before leaving class, record your assignments. If you need to ask questions or clarify directions, do it *before* you leave the classroom. Make sure that you know the due date of every assignment.

✔ AT YOUR LOCKER

Before going home at the end of the day, check your assignment sheet. Get everything you need to complete your homework.

✔ AT HOME

Check your daily schedule, then stick to it. Keep your commitment to study and do your homework at the same time each day, if at all possible.

✔ AT HOME

Before going to bed for the night, put your backpack or bookbag, supplies, books, homework, signed notes, special projects, etc. in one place, preferably the same place every night. This will make it easier to leave for school in the morning.

LISTEN and TAKE NOTES

Listening Habits Inventory

What kind of listener are you? Find out by taking this Listening Habits Inventory.

You'll need a piece of paper and something to write with. Number the paper from 1-12. For each statement, give yourself 2 points if you *always* do it, 1 point if you *sometimes* do it, and 0 points if you *never* do it.

1) I'm in my seat and ready to listen soon after the bell rings.

2) I don't do other things while the teacher is talking.

3) I don't talk with friends while the teacher is talking.

4) I listen carefully to directions.

5) I ask questions when I don't understand directions or other information the teacher presents.

6) I take notes when the teacher presents a lot of information.

7) I know when the teacher is making an important point.

8) If I catch myself daydreaming, I try to get back on track.

9) I look at the teacher when she or he is talking.

10) I concentrate on what the teacher is saying.

11) If someone else is keeping me from listening, I ask that person to stop talking. If this doesn't work, I ask the teacher to help or change my seat.

12) I spend more time listening in class than talking in class.

scoring:

Add up your points.

16-24 points: You're a good listener!

12-15 points: You need to be a better listener!

11 points or less: Huh?

15

> "Know when to listen and you will profit even from those who talk badly."
>
> —Plutarch

LISTENING FACTS:

did You Know that...

● most of the information and directions presented in class are given *orally* by the teacher?

● hearing is NOT the same as listening? Hearing simply means that sounds are coming into your ears, like waves pounding a shoreline. Listening means that you're actually *thinking* about the sounds and trying to *understand* and *remember* their meaning.

● it's very difficult to listen and do something else at the same time?

● you listen better when you look directly at the speaker?

● you listen better when you add personal meaning to what you hear? For example, if the teacher is talking about career awareness, think about the careers of some people you know.

● you listen better when you try to predict what the speaker will say next? For example, if the teacher says, "You are responsible for three experiments," expect to hear descriptions of all three even if the teacher doesn't say, "First..., second..., third...."

five

reasons to take notes

Some people can remember everything they hear. The rest of us need to take notes! Here are five reasons why:

1 Your teacher probably covers information in class that isn't covered in the textbook. If you don't write it down, you won't have it when you need it.

2 Class notes are your best record of what happens during class, and your best source of material for test reviews.

3 Writing things down reinforces what you hear and helps you to remember.

4 Taking notes makes you a more active listener. You're less likely to doze off.

5 Note-taking skills are critical for success in high school and college. You may think you don't need them now, but you'll definitely need them later, and now is the time to learn them.

Note-Taking TIPS

1. Before class

✏ Read your assignment so you're ready to listen.

✏ Review your notes from the last class.

2. During class

✏ Write down the date and title of each lecture.

✏ Don't worry about punctuation or grammar.

✏ Use abbreviations for speed and efficiency.

✏ Don't write down every word the teacher says.

✏ Do write down everything the teacher writes on the board.

✏ Underline, circle, or star anything the teacher repeats or emphasizes.

✏ Don't write more than one idea per line.

✏ Listen for digressions (times when the teacher gets off the subject). It's okay to take a mental break during these—but don't fall asleep.

✏ Write down any questions the teacher asks, since these are likely to appear on future tests.

✏ Don't cram your writing into a small space. Leave room to add more notes later.

✏ Put question marks by any points you don't understand. Check them later with the teacher.

3. After class

✏ Read your notes as soon as possible after class—ideally, within 24 hours.

✏ Reorganize or type your notes, if this will help you to understand and remember them.

✏ Spell out any abbreviations you may not remember later.

✏ Highlight important points in your notes. This will help you to find facts fast when you review for tests.

✏ Jot down any additional questions you may need to ask the teacher.

✏ If you're absent from class, get the notes from a friend.

3 ▷ Ways to Take Notes

There are many ways to take notes. Most good students develop a note-taking style that's comfortable and works for them. If you haven't yet found the right style for you, try these.

free-form

Write one idea per line and leave plenty of blank space. After class, you may want to rewrite, outline, or type your notes. Or use a colored highlighter to mark key concepts and ideas.

Training for Knighthood

for males from noble families

1st step - page (7 yrs.)

away from home

religion, hunting, manners

2nd step - squire (15/16 yrs.)

skills to prepare for war

also learned arts - music and poetry

finally - knighthood! (21 yrs.)

ceremony held in church

sword blessed

knight promised to be virtuous and valiant

the Cornell System

The Cornell note-taking system was invented by Dr. Walter Pauk at Cornell University. Many students from middle school through college have used it successfully. It involves five simple stages: **Record**, **Reduce**, **Recite**, **Reflect**, and **Review**. Think of these as the "five R's."

STAGE 1 RECORD

Divide your notebook page in two columns by drawing a vertical line. The narrow column (about 1/3 of the page) is the RECALL COLUMN. You leave it blank during the lecture. The wider column (about 2/3 of the page) is the NOTE-TAKING COLUMN. Here is where you record your notes during the lecture.

10/25

Training for Knighthood

> only for males from noble families
> page (7 yrs.)
> sent away from home
> learn religion, hunting, and manners
> squire (15/16 yrs.)
> learned skills to prepare for war
> learned arts - music and poetry
> finally knighthood !

STAGE 2 REDUCE

As soon after class as possible (within 24 hours, and certainly before your next class), reduce your notes to as few key words as possible. Write these in the RECALL COLUMN.

10/25

Training for Knighthood

	only for males from noble families
page	page (7 yrs.)
	sent away from home
	learn religion, hunting, and manners
squire	squire (15/16 yrs.)
	learned skills to prepare for war
	learned arts - music and poetry
knighthood	finally knighthood !
	ceremony in church
	sword blessed
	knight promised to be virtuous and valiant

20

STAGE 3 RECITE

Cover the NOTE-TAKING COLUMN with a blank piece of paper. Look at the key words in the RECALL COLUMN. Try to recite all the information you can't see. This self-service mini-test will help you prepare for the real thing.

STAGE 4 REFLECT

After reciting your notes, wait awhile. Then, without looking at your notes, think about the information they contain. Are there any big ideas you need to remember for a test? Do you have any unanswered questions about the information? Are there any really hard parts you need to spend more time on?

STAGE 5 REVIEW

Review your notes from time to time. If you do this on a regular basis, you'll be more than ready for any tests that come along. You may even want to schedule your reviews on a calendar. Here's an example.

SUN			WED	THURS	FRI	SAT
	1	2 Review notes p. 1-10	3	4	5 Review notes p. 1-15	6
7	8	9 Review notes p. 1-20	10	11	12 Review notes p. 1-25	13
14	15	16 Review notes p. 1-30	17	18	19 Review notes p. 1-35	20 Make study cards
21 Study for Test	22 Study for test	23 HISTORY TEST !!	24	25	26	27
28	29	30				

Cornell System Summary ▶

1. Record
2. Reduce
3. Recite
4. Reflect
5. Review

If your teacher lectures from an outline, or if your teacher's lecture follows the textbook very closely, you may want to use a *formal* or *informal* outline style for note-taking.

Use the teacher's organization to order your outline. Keep your notes brief. Don't try to write down every word your teacher says.

Formal outlines can be organized into several levels. Use as many of these as you need, and line up the different levels under each other. Don't start a new level unless you can break it down into at least two parts. In other words, don't start a level 1 unless you're fairly sure you'll also have a level 2.

Title of Lecture
I. Roman numerals for major headings
   A. Capital letters for subheadings
      1. Arabic numerals for important facts
         a. Lower-case letters for related facts and ideas

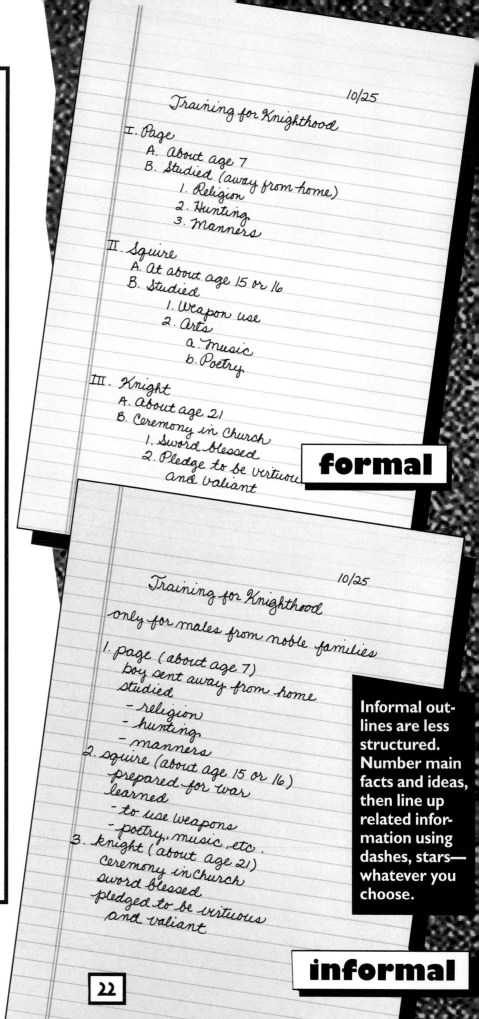

10/25

Training for Knighthood
I. Page
  A. About age 7
  B. Studied (away from home)
    1. Religion
    2. Hunting
    3. Manners

II. Squire
  A. At about age 15 or 16
  B. Studied
    1. Weapon use
    2. Arts
      a. Music
      b. Poetry

III. Knight
  A. About age 21
  B. Ceremony in church
    1. Sword blessed
    2. Pledge to be virtuous and valiant

formal

10/25

Training for Knighthood
only for males from noble families

1. page (about age 7)
boy sent away from home
studied
  - religion
  - hunting
  - manners
2. squire (about age 15 or 16)
prepared for war
learned
  - to use weapons
  - poetry, music, etc.
3. knight (about age 21)
ceremony in church
sword blessed
pledged to be virtuous and valiant

Informal outlines are less structured. Number main facts and ideas, then line up related information using dashes, stars—whatever you choose.

informal

Match Your Notes to Your Teacher's Style

Some teachers follow the textbook, and some don't. Some write outlines on the board, and some don't. Some tell you everything, and some don't seem to tell you anything.

Obviously you can't treat every teacher (and class) the same. For maximum learning and best (test) results, you need to adapt your note-taking style to your teacher's teaching style.

Read the following descriptions of "typical teachers." Think about what kinds of notes you should take for each class. Find suggestions upside down at the bottom of the page.

✍ **Mrs. Vaughn never uses a textbook. Class lectures are her class.**

✍ **Mr. Taylor never refers to the textbook in class. But he always tests you on the textbook material.**

✍ **Ms. Rodriguez follows the textbook exactly.**

✍ **Mr. Masterson follows the textbook sometimes. At other times, he uses his own lecture notes.**

For Ms. Vaughn's class: Take lots of notes; don't rely on your memory alone. You'll be tested on what she says in class. *For Mr. Taylor's class:* Take lots of notes and read your textbook carefully. (For tips on being a better reader, see pages 33–35.) Spend time merging the information from your class notes and textbook. How are they alike? How are they different? Is there conflicting information? Talk to the teacher if your book and his lectures don't agree. *For Ms. Rodriguez's class:* Read the textbook chapter(s) before going to class. Take notes during class. Afterward, reread the textbook chapter(s). *For Mr. Masterson's class:* Keep a complete set of class notes and read the textbook carefully. Spend time merging the information from both sources.

From time to time, it's smart to check the quality of your notes to see how you're doing. Then you'll know if you should make any changes or improvements.

Use this Note-Taking Inventory whenever you feel the need. Simply check it against that day's class notes.

You'll need a piece of paper and something to write with. Number the paper from 1-10. Give yourself 1 point for each item you find in your notes.

1. Date of lecture
2. Title of lecture
3. Writing neat enough for you to read (that's all that counts)
4. No more than one idea per line
5. Plenty of blank space to add extra ideas later
6. All main ideas
7. All important details
8. All key terms and definitions
9. Abbreviations as necessary
10. No unnecessary words

Scoring:

Add up your points.

9-10 points: You're a great note-taker!

7-8 points: You're a good note-taker.

5-6 points: You need to take better notes.

4 points or less: Make a note of this: Practice, practice, practice!

Note-Taking Inventory

YOU HAVE trouble taking Notes

...Compare your notes with a friend's notes. (Pick a friend you know is a good note-taker.) Add to your notes.

...Read the textbook chapter ahead of time. This will help you to be a better listener (you'll already know some of what you hear) and note-taker.

...Talk to your teacher. Explain that you're trying, but it's hard to keep up. Ask the teacher to help you fill in the details.

...If you're really up a creek, ask the teacher if you can tape-record lectures and listen to them later. Then you can take notes at your own speed.

But don't overuse this technique, or you could spend the rest of your life transcribing tapes.

...Keep practicing. Most middle school students are just learning to take notes. Be patient; you'll get better at it.

SPEAK UP

SAY SOMETHING!

Your grade in some classes may depend at least partly on your participation in class discussions. So don't just sit there—say something!

Some students honestly don't know what to say. Others are afraid of saying the wrong thing. Some students fear that if they speak up, others will brand them "know-it-alls" or "Teacher's Pets." Many girls don't want to scare boys off by appearing to be smarter.

If you're worried about any of these issues, start by speaking up in class only some of the time. You may find that others will join in. Once you experience some success, you'll be more comfortable increasing your own level of participation.

Almost anyone can add something meaningful to class discussions. The secret lies in this basic Boy Scout rule: BE PREPARED. If you keep up with your assignments and pay attention to what others are saying, you can make a contribution, too.

CLASS DISCUSSION tips

do...

■ ask legitimate questions based on reading you've done ahead of time.

■ ask legitimate questions about what others say in class.

■ listen carefully to what others have to say.

■ add any information you may have to a point someone else makes.

■ share personal experiences related to the topic being discussed when this will enhance the discussion.

■ make statements or ask questions showing that you came to class prepared.

■ give yourself 3-5 seconds of thinking time before answering a question. Your answers will be more accurate and interesting.

■ be kind when you disagree with what somebody else says.

don't...

■ make comments that take up too much class time.

■ make comments just to hear yourself talk.

■ make a habit of going off the subject.

■ interrupt others.

■ get into arguments.

How to Learn New Words

A bigger vocabulary can help you express your thoughts and feelings more clearly. It can make what you say sound more interesting. It can also improve your performance on tests...and make you a better reader.

We learn new words naturally all the time by listening to our parents, friends, teachers, and TV. With a little effort and a lot of curiosity, you can give your natural learning tendency a push in the right direction.

☞ **Develop word radar.** Become aware of new words as you read and hear them.

☞ **Make an effort to remember new words.** Keep a list in your notebook. Or start a word box with index cards. Write a new word on the front of each card, and the definition on the back. Store your cards alphabetically in a file box. Watch your collection grow.

☞ **If you come across a new word in a textbook you can't write in, jot down the word on a Post-it note and stick it in the book.**

continued on next page

continued from last page

- Try to figure out the meanings of new words from their context—the familiar words and phrases that surround them. If you find a word you can't understand, look it up in the dictionary.

- Use a "word-a-day" calendar in your home study center. Learn each day's new word.

- Use a thesaurus. The root meaning of the word "thesaurus" is "treasury." Think of your thesaurus as a treasury of new words, waiting to be discovered by you.

- Use your head. When someone around you says a new word, ask what it means.

- Be a word detective. Let your curiosity inspire you to learn more about a word than its meaning. Check its pronunciation. Find out where it came from. Examine its roots and track down related words.

- Put on your Sherlock Holmes hat and head for the *Oxford English Dictionary*, called the "OED" for short. Most libraries carry this important reference work. It traces words back through time to their earliest uses, showing how spellings and meanings have changed.

- Become an etymologist—a student of words.

How Diana Lia Learns New Words

Diana Lia is a top-notch student who enjoys learning new vocabulary words. Here's how she does it:

1. First, she makes a list of the new words she wants to learn, with their definitions. **2.** She covers the definitions to see if she can remember them. **3.** She makes a new list of the words and definitions she didn't get right the first time. **4.** She tests herself on this list. **5.** She makes *another*, shorter list.....and on and on until she masters all the words and definitions. **6.** Finally, Diana Lia goes back to her original list an hour or two later. She tests herself on all the words and definitions to find out if she has *really* learned them. If necessary, she goes through her listing-and-testing process again.

"Teach the tongue to say, 'I don't know.'"
—The Talmud

Give Class Presentations

Most people need a great deal of instruction and practice to become skilled public speakers. That's why most high schools and colleges offer courses in public speaking.

Even if you've never taken such a course, you may be required to speak in front of your class. This can be scary, especially without training. You may get stage fright or butterflies in your stomach. Join the crowd! Many experienced speakers report the same symptoms.

Keep in mind that your teacher doesn't expect you to perform like a trained speaker. Class presentations in middle school are mainly warm-up exercises for the more formal presentations you'll give in high school and college. So don't worry about being perfect. Just do the best you can.

PRESENTATION PREPARATIONS

☞ Organize your presentation in the same way you would organize a written paper. Think about your audience, topic, purpose, and format. For tips on preparing a written paper, see page 50.

☞ Brainstorm power-packed openers and closing statements. These are the parts of your speech that your listeners will remember most.

☞ Time yourself. Stick to the time limit your teacher specifies.

☞ Include examples, stories, jokes, and interesting facts.

☞ Use visuals such as charts, graphs, and overheads, but be sure to practice using them ahead of time so you won't fumble during your presentation.

☞ If you don't feel comfortable giving your presentation from memory, ask if it's okay to write it out and read it aloud. Or try speaking from an outline on index cards.

☞ Appearances count. Dress appropriately on the day of your presentation.

presentation practice tips

If you'll be going solo...

● Think about which teachers you like to listen to, and which you don't. Try to figure out what they do that makes you feel this way. Use your observations to plan your own presentation.

● Practice giving your speech in front of a mirror. This will help you to see what your audience will be seeing.

● Practice saying your speech into an audio or video recorder. Afterward, listen and/or watch. Are you going too fast? Are you mumbling? Do you sound excited? Notice areas that need improving.

If you'll be giving your report with a group...

● Make sure that *each* group member is aware of his or her responsibilities. Don't just assume that Ralph will do the summary at the end. Write down *all* of the report-related group responsibilities and assign them to individual group members.

● Practice with your group members, using time limits. Afterward, share suggestions and practice again.

● Practice with visuals and props. For example, you may want one group member to hold up a poster during the presentation. Rehearse this in advance so you don't waste valuable presentation time sorting out who's supposed to do what when.

How to Do Interviews

You can dress up class projects with facts, anecdotes, and information gathered during interviews with experts on the subject.

Interviews can also help you get excited about your project. It's hard to stay bored when you're talking to someone who has made your topic his or her life's work.

For example, if you're studying economics, you may want to interview a family friend who's a banker. If you're studying ecology, try interviewing a neighbor who works with the city water department.

Doing an interview involves more than just asking questions. Follow the guidelines on the next page for a successful experience everyone can enjoy.

> "A person who wants to know will always find a teacher."
> —Persian proverb

29

before
THE INTERVIEW

1. Find someone who has expertise in your subject area.
2. Write or call to make an appointment for the interview. Be sure to:
   - schedule enough time
   - tell your expert why you want to do the interview
   - tell your expert what (if anything) he or she needs to do to prepare for the interview
   - get permission to audiotape or videotape the interview
   - thank your expert in advance for agreeing to do the interview.
3. Before the interview, confirm the appointment date, time, and place.
4. Prepare your questions ahead of time. Include the specific questions you want to ask, plus a few general warm-up questions about the subject. If this is your first interview, ask your teacher to review your questions.

during
THE INTERVIEW

1. Arrive on time or a little bit early.
2. Dress appropriately.
3. Thank your expert for agreeing to do the interview.
4. Act interested and enthusiastic.
5. Start the interview with a few general questions.
6. Follow up with more detailed questions.
7. Listen carefully.
8. Avoid debating with your expert. This isn't the time to argue or make the expert see your point of view.
9. Stay within the time limit agreed upon in advance. Go over only if your expert says it's okay.
10. Thank your expert again at the end of the interview.
11. Offer to show your expert a copy of your interview summary before you turn it in to your teacher. This will allow your expert to correct any misunderstandings.

After
THE INTERVIEW

Write up your summary as soon as possible. Stick to the facts without inserting your personal feelings or opinions. Then write your expert a thank-you note.

BECOME A BETTER reader

WHY YOU NEED to read

You already know that you need to read for school. But that's not the only reason. You'll be reading for the rest of your life. Almost everything you'll ever do—get a job, drive a car, shop, prepare a meal, pay a bill, plan a vacation, figure your taxes, rent a video, raise kids—requires reading skills.

→ Try to think of something that requires *no reading at all*. Video games? (What about the instructions and strategy magazines?) Sports? (How about the ads for the latest basketball shoes, or the stats on your baseball cards?) TV? (You won't know when your program is on if you don't read the TV guide.) Music? (How will you find your way through the CD bins at the store, or read the lyrics to your favorite songs?) The ability to read is your ticket to information. It makes your life richer. It helps you to be a better writer. It satisfies your curiosity and opens your mind. It expands your world and your imagination. It enables you to learn almost anything. It makes you a more interesting person. For more about reading, read on.

31

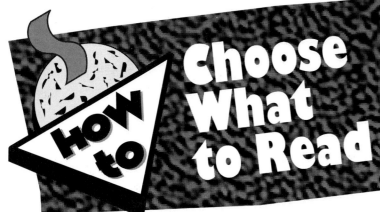

How to Choose What to Read

Have you been to a bookstore lately?

Bookstores in the 90's are lively, colorful, exciting places that offer you thousands of choices. When people say, "I don't read because it's boring," it's often because they haven't found the RIGHT BOOK.

How can you find the RIGHT BOOK? Forget about school projects, book reports, and teacher-pleasing reading. We're talking about the RIGHT BOOK for YOU.

- Start with your interests. Do you like rock music, remote-controlled cars, hair styles, rubber rafting? There are plenty of books on all of these topics.

- No RIGHT BOOK yet? Move on to your needs. Do you need to learn how to play golf, redecorate your room, or research Colorado for your family vacation? You'll find tons of books on any and all of these.

- No RIGHT BOOK yet? Think about your favorite movie or TV show. You'll find novels based on movies, biographies of stars, books about how TV shows and movies are made, and much more.

- Still no RIGHT BOOK? Talk to your friends, an adult you share interests with, and your friendly local librarian. They will all have suggestions to pass on to you.

"The things I want to know are in books. My best friend is the man who will get me a book I ain't read."

—Abraham Lincoln

Take Charge of Your Reading

Teachers can test your understanding of your textbook reading. But their tests only estimate whether you truly understand what you read.

You're the best judge of your own understanding. That's why you need to take charge of your reading. Follow these four steps:

1. Determine the level of difficulty of what you are reading.
2. Develop a plan for reading.
3. Become aware of when you do and don't understand what you read.
4. Know what to do when you don't understand what you read.

STEP 1

DETERMINE THE LEVEL OF DIFFICULTY

You've just turned to today's reading assignment. It's wall-to-wall words, no pictures, and the type is microscopic!

Don't flip your lid. Instead, use FLIP to find out how hard your assignment really is.

FLIP has four categories you complete by answering four questions.

1. F = Friendliness

Question: "How friendly is my reading assignment?"
How to decide: A text is friendly if it has lots of headings, subheadings, words in boldface type, and so on. It's unfriendly if it has few or none of these helpful features.

2. L = Language

Question: "How difficult is the language in my reading assignment?"
How to decide: Choose three paragraphs from different parts of your assignment. Read each paragraph out loud. Are the paragraphs filled with few new words and short, easy sentences? Or do they contain many new words and long, complicated sentences?

3. I = Interest

Question: "How interesting is my reading assignment?"
How to decide: Skim your assignment. (To learn about skimming, see page 38.) If you're interested in the subject, it will probably seem easy to read. If you're not, it will probably seem harder to read and take longer.

4. P = Prior knowledge

Question: "What do I already know about the material covered in my reading assignment?"
How to decide: If you already know a lot about a topic, reading about it will be easy. You'll just be reviewing what you already know, and maybe picking up a few new pieces of information. But if a topic is brand new to you, reading about it will probably be more difficult.

Pages 93-94 contain a FLIP chart you can copy and use to rate your reading assignments. Notice that there are no "right" or "wrong" answers—just your own judgments. Plus you're not trying to figure out what someone else thinks is easy or difficult. You get to decide for yourself.

When you're through FLIPping, add up your ratings and interpret your score. What does it tell you about your assignment? Is the reading level "comfortable," "somewhat comfortable," or "uncomfortable" for you?

Think of FLIP as a set of mental training wheels. Soon you'll be able to figure out an assignment's level of difficulty without FLIP-ping.

STEP 2

DEVELOP A PLAN FOR READING

Take-charge readers figure out their task and make a plan for accomplishing it. Your reading plan should include these three steps:

1. Set a purpose for your reading.

2. Determine an appropriate reading rate, based on your purpose and the level of difficulty.

3. Budget your reading/study time.

Page 95 has a FLIP Follow-Up chart you can copy and use for your reading plan.

1. Set a Purpose for Your Reading

What's your reason for reading a particular assignment? The obvious response is, "Because I have to." But try to be more specific. How about...

☞ for personal pleasure (because you want to)?

☞ to prepare for class discussions?

☞ to answer written questions for class assignments or homework?

☞ to prepare for a test?

Can you think of more? Circle or mark your purpose on the FLIP Follow-Up chart.

2. Determine Your Reading Rate

Is it okay to race through your reading assignment? Or should you stop on every word? That depends on your purpose for reading and how difficult your assignment is.

Circle your reading rate on the FLIP Follow-Up chart.

STEP 3

If your overall rating is...	and your purpose for reading is...	then your reading rate should be...
comfortable	personal enjoyment	RAPID
somewhat comfortable	preparing for a test or for class discussions	MEDIUM
uncomfortable	preparing for a test or for class discussions	SLOW

3. Budget Your Reading/Study Time

Many students crack their books at the start of a study session and stop reading when they're tired. But there's a better way.

"Chunk" the chapter—divide it into small study units. Read and study one chunk, take a break, then move on to the next chunk.

If you're reading a short assignment at a comfortable level, you may be able to finish it in one sitting. But if your assignment is long and/or uncomfortable, chunk it.

Record your reading chunks on the Flip Follow-Up chart. Estimate how long it will take you to read each chunk. Fill in your total estimated reading time.

BECOME AWARE OF WHEN YOU DO AND DON'T UNDERSTAND WHAT YOU READ

You reach the end of a paragraph or page in your book, when suddenly you realize that you didn't understand a word. You don't remember a thing. You've been in the Reading Twilight Zone.

It happens to everybody. But problems come up when it happens all the time and you don't know it—or you don't do anything about it.

You can become aware of when you understand what you read. This is called developing **comprehension awareness**.

Think in terms of "clicks" and "clunks." When something "clicks" in your brain, you understand it. When something "clunks," it's like a loose part on a car. You need to pull over and take a look under the hood.

STEP 4

KNOW WHAT TO DO WHEN YOU DON'T UNDERSTAND WHAT YOU READ

Right after you finish reading a paragraph or page, think "click" or "clunk." If it's a "click," keep on reading. If it's a "clunk," try one of these reading repairs.

- Slow down. Change your reading rate.

- Keep reading anyway. A clue to help you understand may be coming up.

- Reread the paragraph or page.

- Use charts, graphs, tables, pictures, and other visuals to help you out. If there aren't any in the text, create your own.

- If you "clunked" on a new vocabulary word, look it up in your glossary or dictionary.

- Go to another source. For example, maybe you're reading about photosynthesis in your science textbook, and it's too difficult. An encyclopedia article on the same subject might be easier to read. Skim that first, then return to your science textbook.

- Ask a friend, teacher, or parent for help. Getting help when you need it is an important part of being a take-charge reader.

TAKE CHARGE
READING SUMMARY

FLIP to determine the level of difficulty

F = Friendliness
L = Language
I = Interest
P = Prior knowledge

READING PLAN

1. Your purpose
2. Your reading rate (purpose + difficulty)
3. Your reading time budget (chunk & estimate)

COMPREHENSION AWARENESS

"Clicks" and "clunks"

READING REPAIRS

✔ Slow down
✔ Keep reading
✔ Reread
✔ Use visuals
✔ Look it up
✔ Try another source
✔ Ask for help

5 Ways to be an active reader

"I would advise you to read with a pen in your hand, and enter in a little book short hints of what you find that is curious, or that might be useful; for this will be the best method of imprinting such particulars in your memory, where they will be ready, on some future occasion, to adorn and improve your conversation."

—Benjamin Franklin

Some students can read a chapter once and ace a test. Others succeed by reading the chapter several times. But for most of us, reading isn't enough.

We need to **do something** while we read—something that reinforces our reading, helps us to remember what we read, and gives us a way to review our reading later. We need to be **active readers.**

1 OUTLINING

Page 22 lists suggestions for outlining lectures. These work just as well for outlining what you read. Use the author's organization to order your outline. Keep your notes brief; don't copy the whole chapter.

2 NOTE-TAKING

There are several great ways to take notes. Try free-form notes, as described on page 19, or the Cornell System, described on pages 20–21. Or...

➩ Create study flash cards with 3" x 5" index cards. Write a question or key word on the front of each card. Write the answer or definition on the back.

➩ Make study tapes. Record "teacher-like" questions as you read. Pause after each question and record the answer.

SEMANTIC MAPPING

Semantic mapping gives you a verbal picture of a chapter. It illustrates how ideas are organized and related. If you have a strong visual memory, this an excellent way to learn information for tests—especially essay tests.

For example, here's a semantic map on the subject of whales.

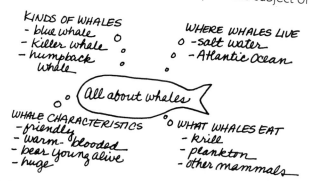

KINDS OF WHALES
- blue whale
- killer whale
- humpback whale

WHERE WHALES LIVE
- salt water
- Atlantic Ocean

All about whales

WHALE CHARACTERISTICS
- friendly
- warm-blooded
- bear young alive
- huge

WHAT WHALES EAT
- krill
- plankton
- other mammals

It doesn't take much to turn these notes into an essay. For example, "There are many different kinds of whales, including the blue whale, killer whale, and humpback whale. Whales are warm-blooded, friendly, and huge! They bear their young alive, like other mammals...."

How to Make a Semantic Map

1. Determine how the author organized the information in the chapter.

2. Write down a main idea and draw a shape around it.

3. Write down secondary ideas (no more than six or seven) and label them.

4. Add important details under each secondary idea. Be concise.

5. When your map is complete, talk yourself through it as if you were answering an essay question.

SUMMARIZING

A summary is a *short* version of the original text that keeps the main message and follows an introduction-body-conclusion form.

How to Write a Summary

1. Read the entire original.

2. Reread and underline important points.

3. Edit your underlined material.

4. Rewrite it in your own words.

5. Edit your version.

6. Check your version against the original.

7. Rewrite if necessary.

ANNOTATING AND HIGH-LIGHTING

If your textbooks belong to you—if you don't have to turn them in at the end of the year—then why not write right in them? You'll have everything you need in one place (text, notes, questions), plus you'll conserve paper!

Use two different writing instruments: a highlighter to mark the text, and a fine-point pen to write in your comments and questions.

How to Annotate and Highlight

1. Highlight new words and major points.

2. Bracket key passages.

3. Write new vocabulary at the top of the page.

4. Star important facts.

5. Write numbers to order things in a series.

6. Put question marks by things you don't understand.

7. Summarize key paragraphs in the margins.

8. Don't write more than the author! Don't overmark! If you find yourself highlighting *everything*, STOP. You're missing the whole point of highlighting.

How to Be a Speedier Reader

Would you like to be able to read faster? Most people would. Speedier reading can reduce study time, boost test performance, and enable you to enjoy more novels and stories.

But it doesn't help to read faster if you don't remember what you read. The trick is to speed up your reading without losing comprehension. You do this by **becoming a flexible reader**, **breaking bad reading habits**, and **practicing**.

GET FLEXIBLE

You can learn to vary your reading rate, depending on what you're reading and why. Here are four different rates to try. (WPM = Words Per Minute.) **TIP:** This page has 329 words on it.

1. **Careful, analytical reading (50-300 WPM).** This is the rate to use for textbook material—stuff you'll be tested on later.

2. **Rapid reading (300-600 WPM).** If the material is easy for you, and if you already know a lot about the subject, and if you're not going to be tested on it, go ahead and read quickly. You may even want to skip some parts. This is the rate to use for magazine articles, newspapers, or books you're reading for pleasure.

3. **Skimming (up to 1,500 WPM).** Preview a chapter, zip through a newspaper article, or race through a magazine piece with this reading rate. Skimming works best when you don't know what you're looking for and you're reading unfamiliar material. Your eyes may stop on a word here or there, or a paragraph that's especially interesting to you.

4. **Scanning (up to 3,000 WPM).** Use this supersonic rate to find a name in a telephone book, a word in a dictionary, a movie in the TV guide, or the answer to a textbook question after you've already read the chapter.

"When I was a kid in Philadelphia, I must have read every comic book ever published. I still read comic books in addition to contracts, novels, newspapers, screenplays, tax returns, and correspondence."

—Bill Cosby

BREAK BAD HABITS

Do you point your finger at every word you read? Do you move your lips? These habits can slow you down.

Instead of pointing at every word, hold a card under every line as you read it. This is a crutch, but it can help you break the pointing habit. (Later you can work on breaking the card habit— but by then you'll probably be reading faster.)

Instead of moving your lips for everything you read, try to stop doing it for easy reading. This will be a positive step toward stopping altogether.

Do you always go back and reread?
Sometimes this can improve your comprehension. But you shouldn't have to read EVERYTHING twice.

If you reread too often, try being a more active reader. Highlight or take notes. Do something! This will help to focus your attention so you may not need to reread.

Do you read every word on the page?
Many slow readers do.

It's much faster and more efficient to read in *word groups*. Don't let your eyes stop on every word. Instead, focus on 3-4 words at a time.

For example, here's a sentence from the beginning of this section.

Speedier reading can reduce study time, boost test performance, and enable you to enjoy more novels and stories.

If this is how you would normally read it...

Speedier — reading — can — reduce — study — time, — boost — test — performance, and — enable — you — to — enjoy — more — novels — and — stories.

...try mentally breaking it up into word groups...

Speedier reading/ can reduce study time,/ boost test performance,/ and enable you/ to enjoy more/ novels and stories.

Notice that your eyes stop only 6 times instead of 18 times. Naturally, you read faster.

PRACTICE

- ☞ Try the four reading rates with different materials. Get a feel for each one. You'll soon discover which to use when.

- ☞ Mark off 100 words and time yourself when you read. Use a stopwatch, a watch with a second hand, or a kitchen timer. Start with books or articles that are easy for you. Try to remember what you read.

- ☞ Practice rapid reading on a newspaper article, magazine article, or short story. Write a two- or three-sentence summary.

- ☞ Skim a newspaper article or magazine article. Write a one-sentence summary.

- ☞ Scan the telephone book for your name and your friends' names. Scan sports articles for high-action verbs.

- ☞ Read mysteries. Trying to solve "whodunits" will speed up your reading rate.

- ☞ Gradually move on to more difficult material. Try reading your textbook pages a little faster, but make sure that you can mentally summarize each page before you go on to the next.

- ☞ Try word-group reading a newspaper, where the columns are thin and the words group naturally.

How to Read Fiction

Literature includes everything that has ever been written, from comic books to classic novels. It's divided into two main categories: **fiction** and **nonfiction.**

Fiction is writing that comes out of the author's imagination, even though it may be based on real experiences and placed in actual historical or geographical settings. Even biographies—narratives about real people—can be fictional, if they include made-up stories about their subjects' lives.

Reading fiction should be FUN. Think of novels, short stories, myths, and tall tales as personal videos for your mind. You're free to imagine what the scenes and characters look like. You're not limited by someone else's ideas. (Luckily, most fiction doesn't have pictures.)

From time to time, you may be required to read fiction in school. Some teachers provide outlines or guidelines describing what they expect you to look for. These may seem boring, but they're not all bad. They can make you a better reader by focusing your attention. They can prepare you to participate in class discussions and perform well on tests.

On pages 97–99, there's a literature study guide you can copy and use. Fill one out the next time you read a work of fiction. See if it helps you to understand and remember more of what you read. It will come in handy for reviews, too.

"When I read, I am born into other lives. It's like taking a trip through time. When I read, my head explodes with information and when it settles back down in place, everything is better."

—Richard Dreyfuss

How to Read Nonfiction

Nonfiction is writing that is factual in nature. Textbooks, encyclopedias, newspapers, and many biographies and autobiographies are examples of nonfiction literature.

Most of what you read in school will be nonfiction. Except for literary anthologies, all textbooks fall into this category.

Textbook chapters are loaded with facts. It's up to you to pick out the most important facts, think about how they relate to one another, and remember them in the future. This takes careful, analytical, s-l-o-w reading.

You can't treat a textbook chapter like a story or a magazine article. If you do, you'll miss too much. Instead, you need to budget enough time to read the chapter carefully, analytically, and s-l-o-w-l-y. Don't plan to finish a whole chapter in just a few minutes, unless it's a *very* short chapter.

Sounds deadly, right? Don't worry. Here's a mental exercise to make it more manageable.

Textbook Baseball

What do reading a textbook chapter and playing baseball have in common? Both take time and patience. Follow this game plan to win the World Series of reading.

The Warm-Up

You're sitting at your desk with your textbook open in front of you. But your mind isn't on the chapter ahead. Instead, it's on what you ate for dinner...or what's on TV later tonight...or what you plan to say to your best friend when he or she calls....You need a reading warm-up!

1. Read the chapter title.
2. Read the headings and subheadings.
3. Look at the illustrations and read the captions.
4. Read the introduction.
5. Read the summary and questions.

The Wind-Up

Turn each subheading into a question. This will start you thinking about what information each section will contain.

Examples:
— Subheading: "Causes of the Civil War"
— Wind-up question: "What were the causes of the Civil War?"
— Subheading: "Simple Machines"
— Wind-up question: "What are the types of simple machines?"

The Pitch

Read each chapter section. Keep your wind-up questions in mind. Look for the answers.

The Hit

Answer your wind-up questions. Try to make each one a hit. If you can't think of an answer...**steee-rike!** Try again. Reread that chapter section to find the answer to your question.

The Run

After you've read each chapter section, go back and review your wind-up questions and answers. This will add up to a run—you'll score! And you'll score on a test, too.

Read the Classics

Classics are books that have stood the test of time. They have been read and loved for many years. Many have been made into comic books, cartoons, and movies, because people never get tired of them.

Huckleberry Finn, Alice's Adventures in Wonderland, Oliver Twist, Dracula, Gulliver's Travels, Treasure Island, The Odyssey, Robin Hood, Rip Van Winkle—all are classics, still worth reading.

You may decide to read them on your own. Or your teacher may decide for you. Either way, you'll face the same problems.

The language may be difficult. Sentences may be long. Vocabulary may be unfamiliar. The authors may use outdated expressions or figures of speech. References that made sense to people of that time may not make sense to you.

Don't give up or get discouraged. Instead, try these tips.

- Don't read in bed. Reading the classics takes concentration.
- If you have a choice, start with something familiar. Have you seen the movie of *Treasure Island?* Then you know the story. Now read the book.
- Read something about the author—for example, a brief encyclopedia article. Find out about his or her life and times. This will help you to understand the book a little better.
- Read in big chunks. Plan to spend an hour or so at a time just reading. This will help you to get into the book.
- Don't get frustrated by the big words. Keep reading and try to get the big picture.
- Plan to reread the book in the future. It will feel like visiting an old friend.

Follow Written Directions

Some people would rather do anything than follow written directions. This can get them into trouble at school.

If the directions for your social studies paper say, "Leave a 2-inch margin at the bottom," and you leave a half-inch margin, you could lose points. If the directions for your math final say, "Circle the right answer," and you cross out the wrong answers, you could fail the test. It may not be fair, but it's a fact.

Here are written directions on how to follow written directions—can you follow them?

1. **Read the whole set of directions slowly and carefully, out loud if you can, silently if you can't.**
2. **Underline, circle, or highlight the actions you'll need to take.**
3. **If the steps aren't already numbered, identify and number them yourself.**
4. **Try to imagine the steps in your mind before you actually start working.**
5. **When you have finished following the directions, retrace your steps. Make sure you have followed the directions *completely* and *correctly*.**

Be a Critical Reader

Take-charge readers don't just read the text. They don't just comprehend what they read. They also make personal judgments about the author's message and ideas. They are **critical readers**.

Critical reading doesn't mean pointing out mistakes. Instead, it involves carefully examining what's being said, how it's being said, and who's saying it.

It also involves comparing what you read to what you already know. Let's say you're an expert on Tyrannosaurus Rex. You've been reading about your favorite dinosaur since you were six years old. Now there's a new book out, *T. Rex: The Total Truth!* Because this is a subject you know a lot about, you'll be a good judge of whether the book is worth reading.

Try these critical reading techniques on a newspaper editorial or a controversial magazine article.

- Read the passage from beginning to end. Get a general idea of the author's message.

- Find evidence for the author's qualifications to write on this subject. Is he or she an expert? How do you know?

- If possible, find out who paid the author to write the passage. Does he or she work for the newspaper, a special-interest group, or a public relations firm? What difference does it make? You decide.

- What do you think was the author's reason or purpose for writing this passage?

- Identify three or four facts presented in the passage.

- Identify three or four opinions presented in the passage.

- Answer these questions for yourself: Does the author present both sides of an issue evenly? Or does he or she seem to be biased in one direction?

- Find any words the author used to get you emotionally involved with the issue.

- Decide whether you agree or disagree with the author. Be ready to explain the reasons for your decision.

DO YOU KNOW PROPAGANDA WHEN YOU SEE IT?

Critical readers keep their eyes peeled for propaganda. Propaganda is writing that tries to persuade you to behave or believe a certain way. Look for examples of these propaganda techniques in advertisements, articles, and essays.

testimonials.
A famous person tells you how wonderful a product or idea is.
("I use it because....I think this way because....")

bandwagoning.
The writer suggests that "most people" are in favor of a product or idea—and you'll be "left out" if you don't agree.

glittering generalities.
"New and improved!"
"More than before!"
"Extra strength!"

"plain folks."
The writer uses informal, "at home" language.
"Like you, I believe that...."

name calling.
"The senator is a racist because...."

appeals to prestige.
"Dare to be different...."
"You're not the average person...."
"Only a very few people are privileged to...."

emotional language.
"Mom, the flag, and apple pie..."
"Act quickly—before it's too late...."
"This little girl has never had a new toy...."
"You may already be a winner!"

10 Ways to Sharpen Your Reading Skills

1. Set aside time each day for silent reading of things you're interested in.

2. Read aloud to a younger child—a brother or sister, a neighbor, or a child you babysit.

3. Be curious about new words. The more you learn, the better reader you'll be.

4. Watch educational TV shows and videos.

5. Be a take-charge reader. Determine the level of difficulty of each reading assignment. Develop a plan to complete it.

6. Be aware of your level of understanding. Remember "Click" and "Clunk." Use reading repairs for "clunks."

7. Be a flexible reader. Practice reading at different rates (slow and careful, rapid, skimming, and scanning).

8. Visit the library often. Keep track of the books you read in a reading log. For each, list the title and author, write a brief summary, then add your thoughts and opinions of the book. Note any problems you had while reading it and how you handled those problems. A spiral-bound notebook makes a fine reading log.

9. Vary your reading. Don't limit it just to books or comic books. Try magazines, newspapers, catalogs, encyclopedias, dictionaries, etc.

10. If you have trouble with your reading, tell your teachers. Tell your parents. Get help! This is part of being a take-charge reader.

WRITE RIGHT

Writing one step at a time

Test answers and telephone messages. Notes and journals. Lists and letters. Papers and reports.

Like it or not, there are times when you have to write. Some middle schools require a lot of writing. Your writing load will only increase in high school and college, so it's best to learn the basics now.

Picture each writing assignment as a stairway. Each step you take will bring you closer to GETTING IT DONE.

edit for spelling, punctuation and grammar

revise your writing

put something down on paper

think about and plan your writing

How to Get Started

PICK A TOPIC

1. What are you interested in learning more about?
2. Will you be able to find information about it?
3. Does your topic meet your teacher's requirements?

If you pick something you really want to learn about, you can probably make it fit your teacher's requirements. Your teacher may be more flexible if you show that you're genuinely committed to your topic.

TIP: Be specific. A paper on "Building an Igloo" is easier to write than "A History of World Architecture from the Beginning of Time to the Present Day."

CHOOSE A PURPOSE

Why are you writing? "My teacher made me do it" may be the truth, but it's not much to go on. Instead, try one of these.

- to explain
- to describe
- to tell a story
- to entertain
- to express your feelings
- to persuade

This gives your writing a sense of direction. If you know where you're going, you're more likely to get there.

FIND A FORM

What form will your writing take—essay, story, poem, letter, report, or something else? Has your teacher given you specific instructions, or are you on your own? Ask if you're not sure.

Sometimes a story wants to turn into a poem. Sometimes an essay wants to turn into a story. Find out if you're free to be flexible.

IDENTIFY YOUR AUDIENCE

If you're writing a TV script for teenagers, you can use contractions and current slang. If you're writing a letter to the editor of your city newspaper, you must be more formal.

Who are you writing to or for? Who is your reader? Your mom, your teacher, your friend, the school newspaper? Keep your audience in mind while you write. This helps you to choose the right words, sentence difficulty, and emphasis. It helps you decide on your style and tone.

What if You Hate to Write?

● Make sure that your topic is interesting to you—if not a lot, then at least a little. Keep an open mind. It may get more interesting, if you give it a chance.

● Don't procrastinate! You'll still have to write that paper, even if you wait until the night before.

● If you have a computer (or access to a computer), use it to write on. See page 62 for reasons why.

● Set a goal and plan to reward yourself when you reach it. For example, "When I get my rough draft done, I'll watch my video of 'King Kong Meets Godzilla.'"

● Try freewriting, described on page 49.

● Try the writer's block busters on page 59.

Writing Warm-ups

Once you've picked your topic, use these strategies to get your brain in gear.

☞ **Read** something about your topic.

☞ **Talk** to other people about your topic.

☞ **Brainstorm** about your topic. Quickly write down as many ideas as you can that are related to your topic. Don't stop to think about whether your ideas are any good. Be creative—be crazy!

☞ **Freewrite on paper** about your topic. Give yourself five minutes to write anything that comes to mind. Don't let your pencil leave the paper. If you can't think of anything to write, then write, "I can't think of anything," until you can—and you will. Freewriting frees your mental powers.

☞ **Freewrite on a computer.** Blacken the screen so you can't read or judge what you write. When you're finished, look at the results. You may find a brilliant idea or two.

Plan Your Writing

Some people can sit down and start writing. The rest of us have to plan what we want to say and how we want to say it.

1. Break down your assignment into small, manageable tasks. Plot these on an assignment sheet. Page 87 has one you can copy and use.

2. Predict how much *total* time your assignment will take. A good guesstimate is about an hour and a half per page. (A 10-page paper = about 15 hours of work.) Plan to finish a bit before your deadline so you'll have extra time if you need it.

3. Be prepared to change your plan as needed. You may find that some tasks take you longer than you thought, while others are done sooner.

4. Put your ideas into some kind of rough organization. This will help you decide on the order you'll present your information, what information doesn't fit, and where there are holes you need to fill with more information.

diagrams

Diagrams can help you see how your information fits together. Your assignment may not need as much detail as these diagrams show, or it may need more.

BUBBLES

Put a few ideas or facts in bubbles, one bubble each. Connect them in ways that make sense to you. Once you've filled a few bubbles, you'll get ideas for new ones to add.

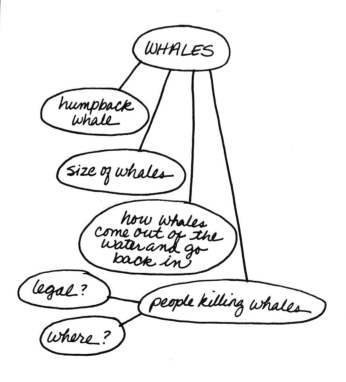

FLOW CHARTS

A flow chart shows how ideas follow one another. Write your ideas or facts in boxes, join them with arrows, then look them over. Are there any information gaps that need filling in? Should you change the order of your ideas?

CAUSE & EFFECT

Cause-and-effect diagrams show how one event leads to another. Write your causes in circles, your effects in squares. Some ideas and facts can be both causes and effects. Draw as many cause-and-effect diagrams as you like, and combine them in the way that works for you.

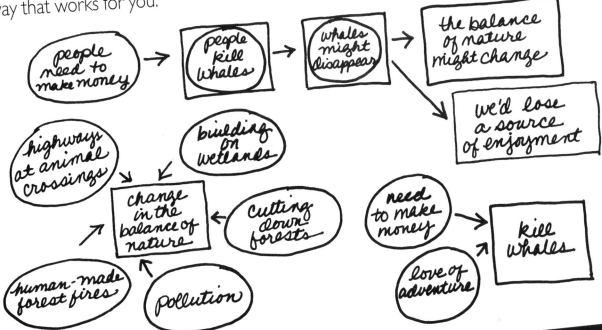

COMPARE & CONTRAST

How are two things the same? How are they different?
A compare-and-contrast diagram can give you some answers.
Look at the information in the section where the two circles meet.
This might make a good starting-point for your paper.

whales

dolphins

- larger than dinosaurs
- sometimes beach themselves
- bone carved into scrimshaw

- like porpoises
- plays with wake of ships
- caught in tuna nets

- mammals
- live in water
- trained to entertain
- communicate by sonar

SEMANTIC MAP

Page 37 tells you how to use a semantic map to take charge of your reading. You can also use it to organize information for a writing assignment.

- Start with a topic.
- Think of possible categories about your topic.
- Find information to fit the categories. Be flexible—you may want to take out some categories and add others.

OUTLINE

Page 22 lists suggestions for outlining lectures. These work just as well for outlining a writing assignment.

An outline is a tried-and-true way to organize information. The more detailed your outline is, the easier it will be to connect your facts and ideas and create paragraphs.

Write a First Draft

You've picked your topic, purpose, and form. You've identified your audience. You've organized your facts and ideas. You can't put it off any longer. Start writing!

✍ Don't worry yet about spelling, punctuation, or "getting it right." Just get your ideas down on paper.

✍ For easier organizing and revising, use a computer or a word processor.

✍ If you have trouble starting at the beginning, jump in anywhere. Write down a point you want to make. Then add sentences to introduce your point, and sentences to support it. Before you know it, you'll have a complete paragraph.

✍ Double space or skip lines to leave room for revisions.

✍ Follow your writing plan for as long as it works. Remember that you can change it if and when you need to.

"The art of writing is the art of applying the seat of the pants to the seat of the chair."

—Mary Heaton Vorse

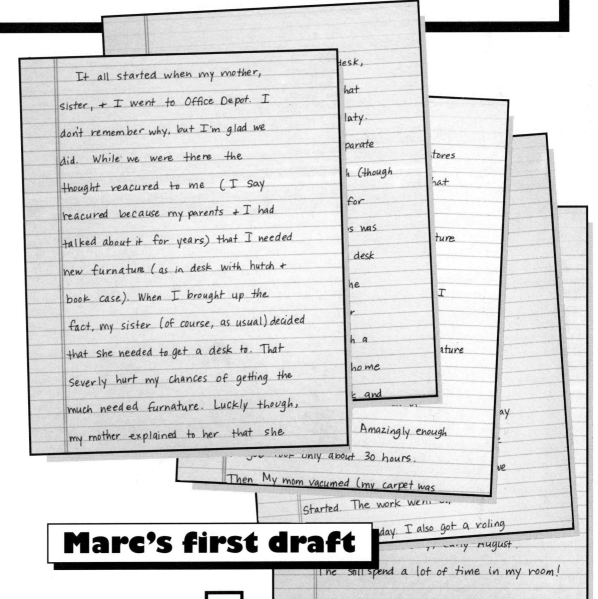

It all started when my mother, sister, + I went to Office Depot. I don't remember why, but I'm glad we did. While we were there the thought reacured to me (I say reacured because my parents + I had talked about it for years) that I needed new furnature (as in desk with hutch + book case). When I brought up the fact, my sister (of course, as usual) decided that she needed to get a desk to. That severly hurt my chances of getting the much needed furnature. Luckly though, my mother explained to her that she

desk,
hat
laty.
parate
h (though
for
s was
desk
he
r
h a
ho me
k and

tores
hat
ture
I
ature

ay
ve

Amazingly enough
only about 30 hours.

Then My mom vacumed (my carpet was
Started. The work went ...
day. I also got a roling
August.
The still spend a lot of time in my room!

Marc's first draft

53

How to Revise and Edit Your Writing

Even professional writers need to revise and edit their writing. Nobody gets it 100% right the first time.

A-OK is a five-part process for finding and fixing problems. If you can remember MOK, POK, SOK, WOK, and NOK, you can master this easy way to write right.

Page 101 has an A-OK checklist you can copy and use to edit your own work. Have a family member or friend edit with you or after you. Another person may catch something you missed.

A-OK

MOK (Meaning OK?)
POK (Paragraph OK?)
SOK (Sentence OK?)
WOK (Word OK?)
NOK (Neatness OK?)

MOK (Meaning OK?)

Ask yourself these questions, one at a time. Read your paper out loud after each question or two. Mistakes are easier to catch when you **1)** hear them, and **2)** pay attention to only one thing at a time. Ignore any grammar or spelling errors for now; you can correct them later.

☞ **"Does it make sense?"**   ☞ **"Are my facts correct?"**

☞ **"Is it concise and to the point?"**   ☞ **"Is there an introduction?"**

☞ **"Is it complete?"**   ☞ **"Is there a conclusion?"**

☞ **"Does it say what I really want to say?"**

Repeat this process, reading your paper to a parent or a friend. Often, another person will catch something you missed.

Marc's revisions

way befor a dissatisfied customer could reach across the desk with a knife). That night when we got home

The one I liked best was a business desk.

until 2:00 A.M. Sunday. I also got a roling chair from my Aunt and Uncle, who came over for diner at abought 8:~~15~~ 30 P.M. ~~Though~~ (they said theyed be there by 8. Consaquently diner got cold. ~~and~~ that Saturday ∧stayed up drinking coffee. After helping finish up the bookshelf thay) with my parents from 2 to 3 A.M. I

PART two

POK (Paragraph OK?)

For each paragraph in your paper, ask:

☞ "Is it indented?"

☞ "Is it made up of sentences related to ONE main idea?"

☞ "Is it connected logically with paragraphs that come before or after?"

PART three

SOK (Sentence OK?)

For each sentence in your paper, ask:

☞ "Does it start with a capital letter?"

☞ "Does it end with the correct punctuation mark?"

☞ "Is other punctuation used correctly?" (Check commas, quotation marks, etc.)

☞ "Does it express a complete thought?"

☞ "Is it a complete sentence (not a fragment or run-on)?"

☞ "Do the subject and verb agree?"

☞ "Is its meaning clear?"

Commas separate items in a series, city and state, dates, and greetings and closings of friendly letters.

If I win the lottery, I will buy the most expensive clothes I can find: jeans, running shoes, and jackets.

I was born in Akron, Ohio. My birthday was January 15, 1980.

Dear Chip,
Blah blah blah.

Your friend,
Dale

Exclamation points show excitement!!!!!

Question marks show the ends of questions.

WOW! Can you really bench press 200 pounds?

Periods go at the ends of sentences that don't need an ! or a ?, and after abbreviations.

Dr. Smith and her friend, Mrs. Black, rushed to the rally.

Quotation marks show the beginning and the end of what someone says. Periods and commas ALWAYS go INSIDE quotation marks. Semicolons and colons usually go OUTSIDE quotation marks.

"I won't," he said calmly, in no uncertain terms. "I simply won't." His mother's stony response was "You will"; his father remained silent.

Semicolons separate main ideas, and items in series that already have commas.

Colons go before a list or an example. They are also used in greetings of business letters.

On his incredible sandwich, Dagwood piled cheeses: Swiss, American, and cheddar; vegetables: lettuce, hot peppers, and cucumbers; and meats: ham and turkey.

Dear Sir or Madam:

Parentheses surround extra comments added (like this one) into sentences.

PART four

WOK (Word OK?)

For each word in your paper, ask:

☞ "Is it spelled correctly?"

☞ "Is it capitalized, if it needs to be?"

☞ "Is it used correctly?"

☞ "Is it over-used?" (Have you used it too often in this paper?)

☞ "Is it slang?" (If it is, should it be?)

☞ "Is it the VERY BEST word, or is there another, better word I could use instead?"

My Room And How It
Came To Be

It all started when my mother, sister and I went to Office Depot. I don't remember why, but I'm glad we did. While we were there the thought ~~recured~~ *recurred* to me (I say ~~recured~~ *recurred* because my parents and I had talked about it for years) that I needed new ~~furnature~~ *furniture* (as in desk with a hutch + book case). When I brought up the fact, my

IF YOU'RE NOT SURE ABOUT YOUR S-P-E-L-L-I-N-G

● Use a spellchecker program, if you're writing on a computer that has one.

● Use a dictionary. A regular dictionary may be hard to use, since you need to know how to spell a word before you can look it up. Instead, try one of these special dictionaries. Check your bookstore, or ask them to order a copy for you.

  —**How to Spell It: A Dictionary of Commonly Misspelled Words** by Harriet Wittels and Joan Greisman (Grosset & Dunlap). A word list (no definitions) that includes both correct and incorrect spellings. Look up a word the way you **think** it should be spelled, and you'll find the way it **is** spelled.

  —**The Bad Speller's Dictionary** by J. Krevisky and J. Linfield (Random House). Arranges words alphabetically according to their common misspellings.

● See page 64 for tips on becoming a better speller.

PART five

NOK (Neatness OK?)

By now, you will probably want to copy your paper over again (or print out another copy). Then ask yourself these questions, one at a time, reading through your paper with each question:

☞ "Does it follow the form required by my teacher?" (Typed and double spaced? Written on only one side of the paper? With correct margins? With a cover sheet or title page? In a folder?)

☞ "If it's handwritten, have I used my best handwriting?" (Check size, shape, slant, and spacing of letters.)

Marc's final draft

"The difference between 'the right word' and 'the almost right word' is the difference between lightning and the lightning bug."

—Mark Twain

My Room And How It Came To Be

It all started when my mother, sister, and I went to Office Depot. I don't remember why, but I'm glad we did. While we were there the thought recurred to me (I say recurred because my parents and I had talked about it for years) that I needed new furniture (as in desk with a hutch and a bookcase). When I brought up the fact, my sister (of course, as usual) decided that she needed to get a desk, too. That severely hurt my chances of getting the much needed furniture. Luckily, though, my mother explained to her that she would just have to wait for her desk, but (much to my sister's delight) that rearranging her room was a possibility. I found a desk with hutch and separate bookcase that I liked very much (though earlier I joked

How to Write Paragraphs

- Make sure that all of the sentences are on the same topic. Make sure they're arranged in an order that makes sense.

- Avoid one-sentence paragraphs. Each paragraph should be long enough to develop its topic.

- Does the paragraph go on and on? Maybe you should break it up into two (or more) paragraphs. Maybe you're trying to say too much. Maybe you're wandering off your topic.

- If you're writing a paragraph that explains something, ask yourself, "What would I learn if I were reading this for the first time?"

- If you're writing a descriptive paragraph, ask yourself: "What would I 'see' if I were reading this for the first time?"

Writer's block

Do you have trouble getting started writing? Do you sometimes get stuck in the middle? Many professional writers suffer from writer's block. Here's how some have described it.

HARLAN ELLISON: "It's like being nibbled to death by mice in Philadelphia."

LOUISE GLUCK: "At times we simply have nothing to say."

MARGARET ATWOOD: "The fact is that blank pages inspire me with terror."

STANLEY KUNITZ: "Writers who have never experienced it have something wrong with them."

MADELINE L'ENGLE: "I got so discouraged, I almost stopped writing."

GABRIEL GARCIA MARQUEZ: "All my life I've been frightened at the moment I sit down to write."

What's your description?

Writer's block BUSTERS

1. Copy a few paragraphs or pages from your favorite book.
2. Imitate your favorite writer's style.
3. Try writing in a style that's new to you. How about an adventure? A science-fiction story? A sword-and-sorcerers fantasy? A romance? A Western? A mystery? Explore new ground. You may discover new writing talents.
4. Draw a picture of your writer's block. Use your imagination. It doesn't matter **what** you draw, just **that** you draw. The act of drawing gets your "whole brain" working and stimulates creative thinking.

How to Write Stories

A story should entertain, inform, interest, or amuse your audience. Your readers should care about what happens to your characters.

- **The Setting.** Where does your story happen? When? Give the geographical location and the specific place of each scene (outdoors? in someone's house?). Think about how long your story takes (a single day? many weeks? a hundred years?). Include lots of colorful details.

For example, the story of Robin Hood takes place in Sherwood Forest a long time ago.

- **The Characters.** Tell your readers what your characters look like. Describe their personalities. Most of all, make them interesting!

Is Friar Tuck holy, roly-poly, and humorous? Would you want to go hunting with Maid Marion? What color hair does Robin have, and does he wear green tights or leather pants?

- **The Problem and Solution.** Present a problem and lead up to the solution.

The Sheriff of Nottingham is over-taxing the people of England, a big problem for them. Robin Hood solves it by taking from the rich, giving to the poor—and besting the Sheriff.

- **The Events**. Describe five or six events. Present them in an order that makes sense. (The order you arrange events in is called the **plot** of your story.)

You can't have Robin give to the poor **before** he takes from the rich.

A story map can help you plan your story. On pages 103–104, you'll find one you can copy and use.

How to Write Essays

An essay is a short work of non-fiction. It can be a single paragraph or several pages long. In an essay, you express an idea, give and support an opinion, or develop a theme.

A letter to the editor is an essay. So are some newspaper and magazine articles. So are most papers written in high school and college. When you state your opinion during a conversation, then back it up with facts and information, you are giving an oral essay.

Follow this form for writing essays.

1. FIRST, say what you're going to say (what will your essay be about?).

2. NEXT, say it (the body of your essay).

- Stick to the topic. Even a very long, very neat paper won't make the grade if it doesn't stay on track.

- Make your organization obvious. Use clue words like "first," "next," "on the other hand," "furthermore," "also," "in conclusion," and so on.

- Say what you mean, and mean what you say. Your teacher can't read your mind.

3. FINALLY, say what you said (your conclusion).

See pages 76–77 for tips on writing essay tests.

Write Poems

Poetry is the oldest form of literature. Before people could write—before alphabets were invented—they made up poems and told them to one another. Many cultures preserved their history in long poems, passed down from one storyteller to the next.

You may think that poetry comes with a lot of rules. Some forms do. For example, if you want to write like Shakespeare, you'll need to learn iambic pentameter—a special kind of rhythm. If you want to write limericks, you'll need to know that a limerick is a five-line poem with a definite rhythm and rhyme.

> *There was a young student from Nome*
> *Whose teacher assigned a long poem.*
> *Though he stayed up all night,*
> *This is all he could write.*
> *Here ends the young Nome student's poem.*

In general, a poem expresses a feeling: love, humor, anger, you name it. Most poems have an inner "beat" or rhythm, like a song or a rap.

Poems DO NOT have to be mushy. Shel Silverstein writes funny poems; Jack Prelutsky writes gory poems. Different poets have different "voices," themes, and styles.

Poems DO NOT have to rhyme. As a matter of fact, forcing a rhyme can lead to truly awful poetry.

> *I ate a cake*
> *that Mom had to bake.*
> *What a mistake!*

Mostly, a poem you write must say something **you** want to say. It should speak with **your** voice. Since poems usually have fewer words than essays or stories, you must choose your words carefully. Try many different words until you find the right ones for your poem.

Like other forms of writing, a poem should have a definite topic, purpose, and audience. Your teacher may assign a specific form—for example, a haiku. Make sure that you understand exactly what kind of poem your teacher expects you to write. Ask to see samples.

If you're free to choose any form you like, try one of these quickies. They may not win any prizes, but they'll get the job done.

adjective poem

1. List four adjectives about yourself. Examples: cool, shy, fun-loving, skinny.

2. List four adjectives about the person you'd most like to be your friend. Examples: outgoing, friendly, athletic, popular.

3. Now stack your adjectives like blocks:

> *cool*
> *shy*
> *fun-loving*
> *skinny*
> *outgoing*
> *friendly*
> *athletic*
> *popular*

prepositional poem

1. Make a list of prepositions:

In	Over
Under	Beneath
On	Near

2. Turn each one into a phrase:

> *In the dark woods*
> *Under a maple tree*
> *On the grass*
> *Over the hill*
> *Beneath the bright blue sky*
> *Near home*

Don't be shy. Let yourself go! You may think that poems are impossible to write. In fact, poetry gives you more freedom to experiment and play with words than almost any other kind of writing.

"found" poem

1. Look through magazines and newspapers for words and phrases that catch your eye.

2. Cut them out and arrange them on a piece of paper. Move them around until you like what you see.

3. Paste them down for posterity.

Feeling the Heat

OUCH!

Neck-Deep

Hot As
A Pistol

feed the flames

Such Sweet Sorrow

How to Write a Book Report

First, READ THE BOOK. Accept no substitutes. Don't settle for the movie, or the comic, or a friend's book report. The book is the real thing.

Next, follow the format your teacher gives you. If your teacher doesn't provide specific instructions, copy and use one of the forms on pages 105–110.

Or try one of these fun alternatives. Clear it with your teacher ahead of time.

- Make a book jacket. Create art for the cover. Write copy for the back and the flaps.

- Write a sequel or prequel to the book. What do you think happens after the last page of the book? What do you think happened before the first page?

- Create a collage about the book.

- Make a poster advertising the book.

- Write a slogan promoting the book.

- Design a T-shirt about the book.

- Come up with your own idea.

Should You Write on a Computer?

If you have one (or access to one), use it! Depending on your software, your computer can...

...make it easier to organize, add, take out, and move information,

...check and correct your spelling,

...center your titles,

...point out errors in grammar and punctuation,

...hyphenate words correctly,

...set margins all around your paper,

...do illustrations, such as pie graphs and bar graphs.

This book was written on a computer, edited on a computer, and designed on a computer. So you can see some of what computers can do.

Still, no computer or software can...

...think, or

...correct spelling mistakes that are real words.

You'll still have to make the decisions about what to write and how to write it. (It may **look** great when it rolls out of the printer, but how it reads is up to you.) And your computer won't change "in" to "on," "no" to "know," "dessert" to "desert," etc. Even so, computers are terrific time-savers.

Write a Research Paper

You walk into class and there it is, in giant letters on the chalkboard:

WRITE A TEN-PAGE PAPER ON GERBILS. DUE IN THREE WEEKS.

It's a big job, but **you've** got to do it. And you'll need to call on most of your School Power skills: getting organized, taking notes, reading, and writing.

☞ Make sure that you understand the assignment. If you don't, ask.

☞ Find out all the requirements for the paper. Will it need a title page? A table of contents? A bibliography? Pictures, illustrations, maps, or other graphics? Should it be typed? Double spaced?

☞ Pick a topic. Even if the teacher assigns the main topic, you should be able to choose your own angle. For example, if the main topic is "Recycling," you may want to focus on aluminum cans.

The trick is to pick a topic that's broad and narrow at the same time. If it's too broad—for example, "The United States"—you'll find so much information you won't know where to start. If it's too narrow—for example, "The Eating Habits of Parakeets in Frostproof, Florida"—you may not find any information at all.

"Research is...poking and prying with purpose."

-Zora Neale Hurston

☞ Turn your topic into a thesis sentence that summarizes what you plan to write about. Examples: "Football is the most popular sport in the United States." "Women aren't paid as much as men for the same kind of work." Have your teacher approve your thesis sentence.

☞ Research your topic in the library. Skim and scan many sources of information. Don't limit yourself to encyclopedias. If you can't find what you need, ask the librarian for help.

CAREFULLY write down your sources. You will need them later for your bibliography.

☞ Contact community resources related to your topic. This is a great way to add originality to your paper. You might collect posters of different countries from a travel agency. Or ask ethnic restaurants for menus. Or learn about a profession by contacting its professional association. Or interview experts in your own community. For interview tips, see page 30.

☞ Write letters to request information from national sources. Find sources and addresses in your library's reference section.

☞ Take notes on the materials you find or receive. Write them on index cards so you can put them in order later.

☞ Plan your paper, using suggestions on page 50.

☞ Write a rough draft, following your plan. Revise your outline if you need to.

☞ Revise and edit your rough draft with MOK, POK, SOK, and WOK from A-OK. See pages 54–58.

☞ Write your final draft with NOK from A-OK.

See pages 111–112 for a Research Paper Checklist you can copy and use.

THE GOLDILOCKS RULE

If you have a tough time coming up with a topic, try this exercise.

1. Brainstorm as many ideas as you can in 5 minutes. Use a timer.
2. Write down all of your ideas. Don't stop to read them or judge them.
3. When the timer goes off, STOP.
4. Organize your ideas into categories with the Goldilocks Rule:
   - (1) = Too Broad
   - (2) = Too Narrow
   - (3) = Just Right
5. Pick a topic from the Just Right category.

SAMPLE bibLiography

Your teacher may give you specific instructions about how to write your bibliography. If not, here's a basic style you can follow.

author

title of magazine article

Allis, S. (1991, July). Do American children need national tests? TIME, pp. 62-63.

title of newspaper article

pages

Film with anti-gang theme opens to rash of violence. (1991, July). The Miami Herald, p. 1.

title of book

Snider, J. (1983). How to study in high school. Providence, RI: Jamestown Publishers.

publishing company

"The best of my education has come from the public library.... My tuition fee is a bus fare and once in awhile, five cents a day for an overdue book. You don't need to know very much to start with, if you know the way to the public library."

—Lesley Conger

How to Be a Better Speller

Some people are terrible spellers. But most of us can learn to be better spellers, if we try.

Being a better speller will make writing easier for you. It will save you time. And when spelling counts as part of your grade, it will earn you points.

- Pay attention to how words are spelled. Do this when you read *and* when you write.

- Keep a personal list of new and difficult words. See pages 26–27 for suggestions.

- Play word games. Try Scrabble, Boggle, UpWords, Scattergories, and Hangman.

- If your family has a hand-held electronic dictionary (some popular ones are made by Franklin), borrow it to play the word games.

- Teachers and other reading specialists have made lists of "spelling demons"—words that seem to give students the most trouble. You'll find two "demon lists" on pages 113 and 114. Make copies for your notebook and the bulletin board in your home study center. Ask your friends and family to practice the words with you. (They make great Hangman puzzles.)

- Set up a schedule for studying spelling words.

SAMPLE
Spelling Study
SCHEDULE

On the day spelling words are assigned...

Test yourself on the words for that week. Find out which ones you'll need to study.

For the rest of the week...

Schedule regular study sessions for every day or every other day. Keep them short—no more than 15-20 minutes. Several short sessions are more effective than a night-before-the-test cram-a-thon.

Squeeze brief practices into spare moments—in the car, while you're waiting to be picked up from soccer practice, on the bus, during breakfast.

On the night before the test...

Review all words—the hard ones and the easy ones.

Get help studying. Have a friend or family member dictate your spelling words to you. Write them down, leaving a blank space after each. Afterward, check your work. For any misspelled word, write the correct spelling under the incorrect spelling.

Or record your own test tape. Dictate your words, leaving a pause after each so you can write it down.

Make up mnemonics—memory tricks—to help you remember spelling words. You already know "i before e except after c." Try remembering "piece" as a *pie*ce of *pie*. See page 71 for more mnemonic examples.

Write *all* of the spelling words that give you trouble. Then write them again and again until you've mastered them. Don't count on remembering words you only spell out loud. You need to write them.

Use computer programs like Crossword Magic to create crossword puzzles from your spelling words.

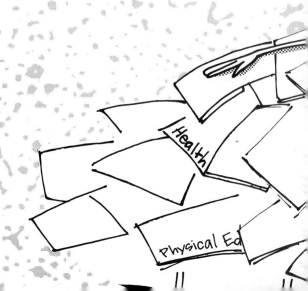

STUDY Smarter

How to Study

Adults talk about two facts of life they can't escape: death and taxes. Two facts of school life come close: tests and homework.

You can run, but you can't hide. And unless you're a genius, there's just one way to make the grade. Buckle down, get down and study.

- Post your DO NOT DISTURB sign.
- Look over everything you need to do, and write a study plan.
- If you have a lot to study, plan several short sessions with breaks. You'll be more productive.
- Is there anything you'll need help with? Tell your study partner or parent. Schedule time together. DON'T wait until the last minute.
- Do the tough assignments first, when you're fresh.
- Vary your study activities. Read for awhile, then write, then do math problems, then memorize, then read again.
- Save the last few minutes for a final review of test material or material you need to memorize.

Do you have trouble remembering what you study? See page 71 for memory boosters.

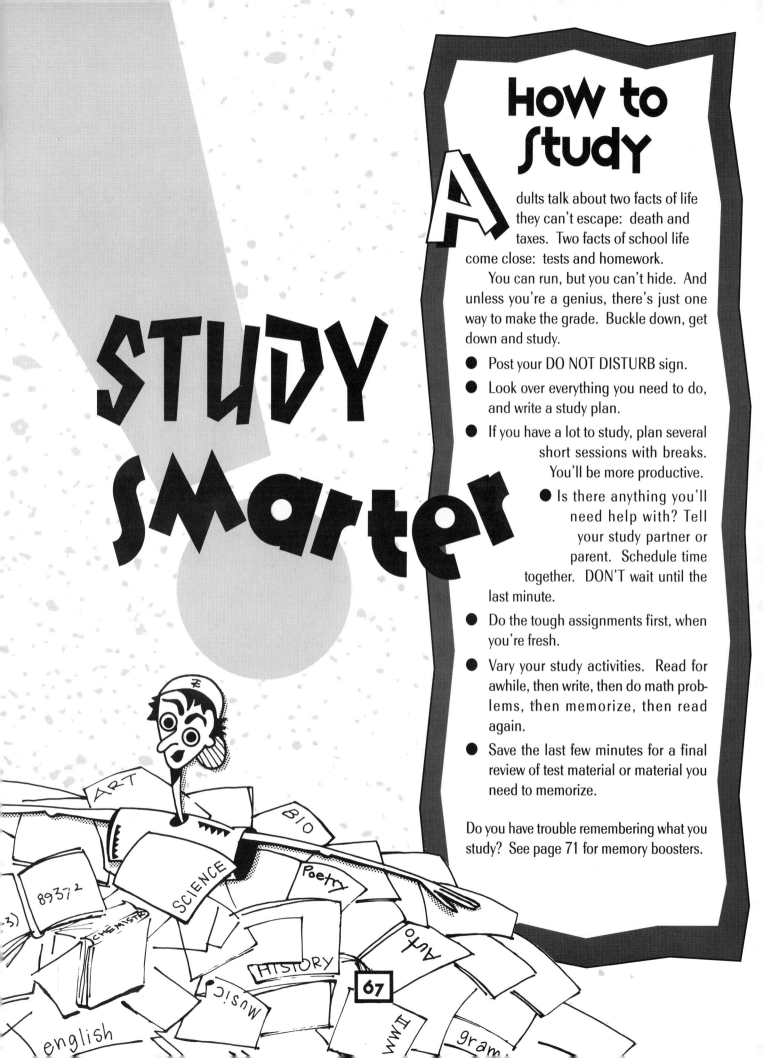

Study Plan Practice

You have six assignments to complete tonight. What order will you do them in? Why?

___ **Work 10 long division problems and 3 word problems.**

___ **Study a chapter for a science test.**

___ **Write a short story for English class.**

___ **Read a chapter for social studies.**

___ **Ask your parents to sign the permission form for your class field trip.**

___ **Define 15 words for computer science.**

7 WAYS to improve your concentration

Some people can concentrate for long periods of time. But even if your attention span is short, you can keep your mind on something you're **really** interested in. And you can improve your ability to concentrate if you're willing to work on it.

1 Follow the suggestions on pages 2–3 for setting up a home study center. Try to make your study center a special place *only* for studying—no noise, toys, or distractions.

2 Start with short study sessions. Increase your study time by 5-10 minutes each day until you reach your goal.

3 Set small goals and reward yourself when you reach them.

4 Try your hardest to get interested in what you're studying. If a subject is boring to you, find a friend who likes it and ask why. Read a magazine article or watch a video about it. Come up with questions to ask your teacher in class.

5 Some of us are "larks"—morning people. Some of us are "owls"—night people. Owls hate to study in the morning, and larks fall asleep at night. What's your peak time? Study then.

6 Keep active. Take notes, underline, write down questions, highlight, draw diagrams, read aloud, and ask yourself questions.

7 If you start to fade or daydream, stop. Stand up, stretch, jump up and down, munch an apple—or take a short nap, if you really need it.

How to Start a Study Group

Many students like to study with their friends. It's less lonely and more fun. Plus a study group can help everyone do better on tests—as long as all members do their share of the work.

✔ Limit your group to 3 or 4 students. Pick students who stay awake in class, ask questions, and take notes.

✔ Give the group a try-out with a one-time-only study session. If it seems to work, plan another session or set a regular meeting time.

✔ Shorter, more frequent meetings are better than once-a-month cram-a-thons.

BEFORE THE STUDY SESSION

1. Draw up an agenda (meeting plan). Decide what material to cover.

2. Plug each topic into a time frame. For example, 15 minutes for science, 20 minutes for social studies and history.

3. Assign each group member a part of the material to study. It's that person's responsibility to "teach" it to the rest of the group. Your study session will be made up of several "mini-lessons."

4. Get ready to teach your own mini-lesson. Read all assigned material or class notes. Identify any problem areas. Make up test questions to ask the group.

DURING THE STUDY SESSION

1. Start by going over the agenda. Set or review group rules.

2. Ask for a volunteer to be an "agenda monitor." That person will keep track of time and make sure the group doesn't wander off the topic.

3. Go through the mini-lessons. Group members should feel free to ask questions and add material that isn't covered. Each "teacher" should stop every few minutes or so, checking to see that group members understand the material being presented.

4. End each mini-lesson with practice test questions. Brainstorm more questions.

5. End the session by reviewing major ideas and problem areas.

Are your grades not as good as you think they should be? Do you sometimes have trouble on tests? Maybe you need a study check-up.

Page 115 has a form you can copy and use to find out how healthy your study habits are. Fill one out during your next study session. It will help you to see how you're spending your time. Maybe you're skipping something you should be doing. You're the doctor. You decide.

Nick's tip for study groups

Whenever Nick had a group assignment, he and his group usually ended up working in the library. Nick liked this so well that he decided to study in the library with friends, even when their assignments were individual ones. They hold their study group meetings at the library.

How to Remember What You Study

You spend hours studying for a test, alone or in a group. Then the big day arrives, and suddenly your mind is a black hole.

It can happen to anyone. You can help prevent it by adding these memory boosters to your study sessions.

☞ **Recite.** Read aloud. Recite what you are learning to yourself, a study partner, or a parent. Hearing and speaking can help information stick in your mind.

☞ **Use mnemonics.** Make up words, names, or sentences to help you remember facts and ideas.

Examples:

To remember a sequence, use a sentence or key words. For the colors of the spectrum, memorize ROY G. BIV—Red, Orange, Yellow, Green, Blue, Indigo, and Violet.

To remember a date, try a rhyme. ("In 1492, Columbus sailed the ocean blue....")

To remember the meaning of a word, associate it with something you know. For "obnoxious," you might think of the school bully.

☞ **Overlearn.** Keep studying something even after you know it. Overlearning is especially useful if you get very nervous during tests.

☞ **Visualize.** Picture what the information looks like on the page you're studying. Make mental pictures of facts and ideas. Draw real pictures, if that helps you to learn.

☞ **Apply what you learn.** If you use it, you won't lose it.

Example:

If you read a computer manual and then practice the program, you'll remember much better than if you stick just with the reading.

Cathy's tip for remembering

Cathy sometimes had trouble remembering what she read. She started reading aloud to herself. She finds that this helps her to remember more. She may not always want to read aloud to herself, but for now, this technique works for her.

turn learning into a game

Learning is serious business, but it doesn't have to **be** serious all the time. There are many ways to learn besides studying and sitting in class.

Stretch your brain, strengthen your funny bone, build your skills, and add to your knowledge base with these entertaining games. Play with friends and family or challenge yourself. Your study group may decide that a game is a great way to end a study session. Here's a list of commercially available games you may want to try.

BALDERDASH

Builds vocabulary. Players bluff one another by making up phony definitions for real but zany words.
Example: "perwitsky."

ASAP

"The Quick Think Game." Builds vocabulary and trivia knowledge.

THE GAME OF SNIGLETS

Builds vocabulary. Players combine roots to form interesting new words. Examples from the book, **Sniglets**, by Rich Hall: "Cheedle: The residue left on one's fingertips after consuming a bag of Cheetos." "Chalktrauma: The body's reaction to someone running his fingernails down a chalkboard."

CLEVER ENDEAVOR

Builds vocabulary. Players answer clues and riddles to guess a given word.

BOGGLE

Builds vocabulary. A timed game in which players find words in letter combinations.

PILEUP GAME

Teaches stress management skills (less stress lowers test anxiety). Board game shows how stress "piles up" and how creativity improves and expands our abilities to cope.

JEOPARDY

Builds general knowledge. The trivia game based on the TV show. Available as a board game or video game.

OUTBURST JUNIOR

Builds general knowledge. A timed trivia game. Also try the adult version.

QUICK WIT

Builds general knowledge. Players answer questions in vocabulary, math, and "common sense" areas. Includes verbal and visual brain-teasers.

RISK and CASTLE RISK

Builds geography and strategic thinking skills. **Risk** concentrates on world geography; **Castle Risk** on European geography.

TABOO

Builds vocabulary. A timed game in which one player tries to get teammates to guess a word or phrase—BUT there are some words and phrases the player can't say. Examples: You want your teammates to guess the word "sink." BUT you can't use "swim," "kitchen," "water," "disposal," or "faucet" as clue words. You want your teammates to guess the phrase "The World Series." BUT you can't say "baseball," "game," "National League," "American League," or "champions" as clues.

24 GAME

Builds math skills. Add, subtract, multiply, or divide four numbers to arrive at the number 24. This fast-paced game has been featured in tournaments across the country.

UNGAME

Builds problem-solving and communication skills. Players respond to hypothetical social situations.

TRIVIAL PURSUIT & JR. TRIVIAL PURSUIT

Builds general knowledge. Trivia games available in several versions.

WHERE IN THE WORLD?

Builds geography skills. Players learn locations, cultures, and economies of countries around the world. Four levels of play.

WHERE IN THE WORLD IS CARMEN SANDIEGO?

Builds geography skills. A computer software game, available in several versions for many kinds of computers.

73

How to Predict Test Questions

If you can predict the questions your teacher will ask, and if you practice your answers, you **will** do better on tests. The CHANCE strategy can help you predict possible test questions. It's the next best thing to a crystal ball.

C = Critical ideas

Focus on the **critical ideas**—the ones that are most important to understanding the chapter or topic as a whole. Most teachers won't test you on the picky details.

H = Higher-order questions

Some questions require answers that are very clear. You can find the answers right in your class notes or textbook. These are called **lower-order questions.**

For example, "Which president's wife held seances?" "When did the **Lusitania** sink?"

But other questions require more thinking. You have to pull information from more than one sentence or paragraph, make judgments, or draw conclusions. These are called **higher-order questions.**

For example, "What would happen if a president's wife or husband held seances today?" "How might history have been different if the **Lusitania** had not been sunk?"

When preparing for a test, try to predict both kinds of questions.

A = Accuracy

Do you understand the material you're studying? If you can tell in your own words what a textbook chapter said, or explain what your teacher meant during a class lecture, then you are interpreting these materials with **accuracy**. The questions you predict will be more accurate, too.

N = Number

Don't predict just one or two questions. Predict a large **number**—as many as you can. Cover all the material you are studying. The more questions you predict, the more answers you can practice, and the better you'll do.

C = Clarity

Confusing questions lead to confusing answers. Are your questions clear? Do they have **clarity**?

You can improve the clarity of your questions by choosing your words carefully. For example, "What are the five major causes of the Civil War?" has more clarity (and leads to better answers) than, "What are the reasons the Civil War started?"

E = Examine

Use your predicted questions to **examine** yourself. Make up and take a sample test. Check your answers against your textbook and notes.

CHANCE

C = Critical ideas
H = Higher-order questions
A = Accuracy
N = Number
C = Clarity
E = Examine

diana Lia's tip for checking your work

Diana Lia checks her answers with friends before turning in her homework assignments. Sometimes the teacher doesn't get around to correcting all the homework. This way, Diana and her friends at least know if they are on the right track. They aren't so surprised when test time comes.

How to Psych Yourself Up for a Test

It's the night before the Big Test. You've been studying for days. What can you do to get in the mood for tomorrow?

Start by going to bed. Get a good night's sleep. In the morning, eat a healthful breakfast. Save the Sweet 'n' Sticky Belly Bombs for another day so you don't sugar-crash in mid-test. Dress in comfy clothes. Listen to your favorite music while you're getting ready for school.

In other words, take care of yourself. No secrets here!

Before leaving home, make sure you have everything you need for the test. You may want to make a mini-checklist:

___ **Pencils**
___ **Pens**
___ **Paper**
___ **Books (if you can use them during the test)**
___ **Calculator**
___ **(Anything else?)**

Try to arrive a few minutes early. On the way, tell yourself, "I'm ready. I'll do my best—and that will be good enough for me."

75

(See page 71.)

WHEN TO CRAM FOR A TEST

The best time to cram for a test is...

A. the night before
B. the morning of
C. neither

The answer is C. Although it's tempting to leave your studying to the last minute, and you'll probably remember *some* of what you stuff into your brain, you won't remember it for long. You may not even remember it during the test.

Instead of cramming, give yourself plenty of time to review. Start on the day the test is announced.

● Go over everything at least once—textbooks, class notes, old tests and quizzes.

● Memorize lists, formulas, and definitions. Use mnemonics. (See page 71.)

● Pay special attention to problem areas. If possible, get help from a friend or family member.

● Learn the correct spellings of key terms and technical words.

● Make up a sample test. Answer the questions. Check your answers.

5 ways to conquer test anxiety

1. Memorize important facts, figures, formulas, and dates ahead of time. Then, just before starting the test, do a "splashdown" on the back of your paper. Quickly write down anything you think you'll need for the test. Later, if text anxiety creeps in, you'll still have important information at your fingertips.

2. Practice the test-taking strategies in this section. The more prepared you are, the less anxious you'll feel.

3. If you start getting anxious, take a brief relaxation break. Close your eyes. Breathe deeply. Think about tensing, then relaxing every part of your body, from your toes to the top of your head.

4. If other students finish before you do, ignore them. It's a myth that top students finish first, average students finish in the middle, and poor students finish last.

5. If you finish early, use the time to check your answers.

How to Take Essay Tests

Essay tests can be the pits. First you have to understand the question. Then you have to figure out the answer. Then you have to remember information that fits the answer. Then you have to organize it in a way that makes sense. Then you have to write it down. And all within a time limit!

You can't escape essay tests. But you can make them easier to take.

BEFORE THE TEST

Practice PORPE, a five-step way to prepare for essay tests on any subject.

1. P = PREDICT
Predict test questions using the CHANCE strategy on page 74. Ask your friends or study group to predict questions. The more questions you come up with, the better.

2. O = ORGANIZE
Organize the information needed to answer the questions. Use diagrams, outlines, charts—whatever works. See pages 50–52 for ideas.

3. R = REHEARSE
Review the memory boosters on page 71. Recite the information in your diagrams, outlines, or charts. Repeat over the next several days so the information sticks in your long-term memory.

4. P = PRACTICE
Practice writing the answers to your predicted questions. Time yourself to model test conditions. Quickly jot down important ideas, and sketch your diagrams, outlines, or charts from memory. Add examples and facts to back up your ideas.

Because your teacher may give you different types of essay questions, practice writing different types of answers. Examples: "Discuss...." "Explain...." "Describe...." "Compare and contrast...."

Check the overall organization of your answers. For each, is there an introduction? A conclusion? Does it make sense? Have you included all major points? Have you said what you really wanted to say?

5. E = EVALUATE

Go over your answers with a teacher's eye. How could they be better? What have you forgotten? What have you done especially well?

Evaluating answers would be a good activity for your study group to do together.

PORPE

P = Predict
O = Organize
R = Rehearse
P = Practice
E = Evaluate

DURING THE TEST

■ Read all of the questions. Do a quick "splashdown" on the back of your paper or a piece of scrap paper. Jot down any names, facts, dates, etc. you think you'll need for your essays. OR brainstorm words related to your topic, and group them in a cluster.

Physical Fitness   **exercise**
eat right
not flabby
good endurance   **sleep enough**

■ Follow directions EXACTLY. You'll stay out of trouble and you may save time.

For example, if you're instructed to "define" or "summarize" a topic, that usually means you can write a brief answer. "Discuss," "explain," or "describe" calls for a longer answer. "Compare and contrast" means what it says: tell how two things are the same, AND how they are different.

For tips on following written directions, see page 42.

■ Write your essay. If you think you have time, write it first on scrap paper, proofread it, make any changes, then copy it onto your test paper.

For tips on writing essays, see page 60.
■ Read your essay to make sure it makes sense.

The STAR Strategy for Test Success

STAR is a simple four-letter formula that's especially useful for timed tests.

SURVEY the test to get an idea of how much time you can spend on each question, and which questions you can answer quickly. Pay attention to the number of points per question.

TAKE time to read the directions CAREFULLY. Studies have shown that poor test-takers tend to misread directions and questions.

ANSWER the questions. Start with an easy one to boost your confidence.

REREAD the questions and your answers. Make any needed changes.

For Taking Objective Tests

There are many different kinds of objective tests—multiple-choice questions, true-false, fill-in-the-blank, matching tests, etc. True-false and fill-in-the-blank are the trickiest.

TRUE-FALSE

- If **any** part of a statement is false, then **all** of the statement is false.

- Watch for absolute words like "all," "none," "only," "always," and "never." They can be clues that an answer is false. Few things are "always" or "never" so.

- Watch for weasel words like "usually," "generally," "often," "seldom," "some," and "may." They can be clues that an answer is true.

MULTIPLE-CHOICE

- Read each possible answer WITH the stem. This will help you focus on the right answer to the question you are given.

Example:

(STEM) Many teenagers like:
(POSSIBLE A. to listen to loud music
ANSWERS) B. to wear clothes that are "in"
C. to be on their own
D. to go to parties
E. all of the above

You would read this question five ways:

- A. (Many teenagers like) to listen to loud music.
- B. (Many teenagers like) to wear clothes that are "in."
- C. (Many teenagers like) to be on their own.
- D. (Many teenagers like) to go to parties.
- E. (Many teenagers like) all of the above.

- Read ALL choices before picking an answer. In the example above, A seems okay, but it's not the BEST answer. E is.

- Use the process of elimination. If you know that B, D, and E are wrong, then the answer must be A or C.

- When in doubt, guess. Your guess may be right; leaving a blank won't be. *Exception:* Some standardized tests have a penalty for guessing. Check with your teacher.

- If one choice is much longer than the rest, and it seems likely to be right, go with it. Longer answers tend to be right more often than shorter answers.

- If two of the choices are exact opposites, pick one of them.

Example:
What happens when you add salt to water before boiling it?

A. It turns the hydrogen in the water to helium.
B. It makes the water boil faster.
C. It makes the water boil slower.
D. It turns to salt crystals.
E. Nothing happens.
B and C are opposites. Pick B.

- When you don't have a clue what the right answer is, pick C first. If you think C may be wrong, pick B or D. Teachers like to sandwich the right answer between other choices, so avoid A and E.

What if

YOU'RE NOT SURE OF YOUR ANSWER?

You read a question and quickly write an answer you *think* is right. But you're not *positive* it's right. What should you do?

Many people would say, "Leave it. Your first impression is best." But a University of Michigan professor says, "Change it."

Dr. Frank Whitehouse did a study on tests turned in by more than 1,000 of his students over the past 10 years. He looked for eraser marks and other signs that students had changed their answers. He found that students changed from wrong to right answers 2.5 times as often as they changed from right to wrong.

After you answer a question, you may find that other questions contain clues to the first question. Or you may remember an important fact later in the test. Or you may just think twice about your first answer, and feel strongly that you should change it. Don't let superstition about "first impressions" hold you back.

What to Do When the Test Comes Back

When the teacher hands your test back, don't just stick it in your notebook or desk. You can learn a lot from a **PTA—Post-Test Analysis.**

✔ Look at each error. Try to figure out why you made it. Was it a careless mistake? Did you forget to study something, or forget something you studied?

✔ Find out the right answer for each question you missed. Write it on your test paper. Turn it into a study tool for next time.

✔ Keep a file of old tests. They can help you predict the kinds of questions your teacher likes to ask.

Survive Standardized Tests

Standardized tests are a pain. Why should you have to take them? Because many adults feel the need to evaluate you and your school. Standardized tests compare your performance to that of other students in your district, state, or country.

You can try to prepare for standardized tests. You can work on improving your vocabulary all year long. (See pages 26–27 for tips on learning new words.) You can take practice tests at school. Or you can decide not to worry about standardized tests until you have to take them. Then just do your best, and forget about them afterward.

● Use the techniques for conquering test anxiety on page 76. Reread the section, "How to Psych Yourself Up for a Test," on page 75. Review the tips for taking multiple-choice tests on page 78.

● Most standardized tests use a test booklet and a special answer sheet. You fill in bubbles on the answer sheet. There are many questions, so you should make sure that the question number matches the answer number you're filling in. It's easy to lose track.

● If you are right-handed, keep your answer sheet on the right side of your test booklet. This way, you won't waste time crossing your hand over your test booklet after each answer.

● If you are left-handed, keep your answer sheet on the left side of your test booklet for the same reason.

● If you change your mind about an answer, erase your mark carefully, and don't leave any stray marks on the paper. Standardized tests are scored by machines that don't know the difference between filled-in answers and accidental pencil marks.

● Reading comprehension tests almost always have "main idea" questions. These may be disguised as "most important" questions or "topic" questions. As you read, keep an eye out for key main ideas, especially at the beginning and/or end of each paragraph.

Standardized tests are only **one** measure of how you're doing in school. Your day-to-day work is a much better measure. Most teachers know that. So don't stay awake nights thinking about standardized tests. Focus on keeping up with your homework, read a lot, and do your best on classroom tests. You'll do just fine.

TOOLS for SCHOOL Success

time management chart

	Monday	Tuesday	Wednesday	Thursday	Friday	Saturday	Sunday
8:00							
9:00							
10:00							
11:00							
12:00							
1:00							
2:00							
3:00							
4:00							
5:00							
6:00							
7:00							
8:00							
9:00							
10:00							
11:00							

85

Copyright © 1992 by Jeanne Schumm and Marguerite Radencich,
SCHOOL POWER, Free Spirit Publishing Inc. This page may be photocopied.

ASSIGNMENT SHEET

week of:

date of assignment	subject	book or project	page	date due	grade

Copyright © 1992 by Jeanne Schumm and Marguerite Radencich,
SCHOOL POWER, Free Spirit Publishing Inc. This page may be photocopied.

project plan

1. Decide on a project theme.   DATE DONE_____

2. Have the theme approved by your teacher.   DATE DONE_____

THEME: _____

3. Make a list of things you need to do to complete your project. Rank them in the order they should be completed.

_____ _____   _____ _____
_____ _____   _____ _____
_____ _____   _____ _____
_____ _____   _____ _____

4. Decide if you will need help from your parents or other adults. Ask if and when they can help you. Be clear about what you want them to do.

WILL NEED HELP WITH: **WHO WILL HELP ME:**

_____   _____
_____   _____
_____   _____
_____   _____
_____   _____

5. Set deadlines for finishing each part of your project. Write the deadline dates on your calendar.

TASK	DATE DUE	DATE DONE	PERSON RESPONSIBLE

Copyright © 1992 by Jeanne Schumm and Marguerite Radencich,
SCHOOL POWER, Free Spirit Publishing Inc. This page may be photocopied.

6. Make a list of materials you will need. Estimate how much they will cost.

ITEM	COST
_____	_____
_____	_____
_____	_____
_____	_____
_____	_____

7. Send away for resource materials.

RESOURCE MATERIAL	DATE REQUESTED	DATE RECEIVED
_____	_____	_____
_____	_____	_____
_____	_____	_____
_____	_____	_____
_____	_____	_____

8. Contact community resources.

COMMUNITY RESOURCE	DATE CONTACTED	RESULT(S)
_____	_____	_____
_____	_____	_____
_____	_____	_____
_____	_____	_____
_____	_____	_____

9. Visit the library.

PURPOSE OF VISIT	DATE OF VISIT
_____	_____
_____	_____
_____	_____
_____	_____
_____	_____

10. Complete your project on schedule.

DATE TURNED IN: _____ **GRADE:** _____

Copyright © 1992 by Jeanne Schumm and Marguerite Radencich,
SCHOOL POWER, Free Spirit Publishing Inc. This page may be photocopied.

Go For It!

MY GOALS FOR THE SCHOOL YEAR!

today's date:

_____

My goals for the school year:

1. _____

2. _____

3. _____

Reasons why I CAN achieve my goals:

1. _____

2. _____

3. _____

Reasons why I MIGHT NOT achieve my goals:

1. _____

2. _____

3. _____

Ways I CAN overcome or solve these problems:

1. _____

2. _____

3. _____

Copyright © 1992 by Jeanne Schumm and Marguerite Radencich,
SCHOOL POWER, Free Spirit Publishing Inc. This page may be photocopied.

MY GOALS FOR THE SCHOOL YEAR!

Go For It!

UPDATE

today's date:

_____

New or changed goals:

1. _____

2. _____

3. _____

Problems I overcame or solved:

1. _____

2. _____

3. _____

Other successes so far:

1. _____

2. _____

3. _____

Copyright © 1992 by Jeanne Schumm and Marguerite Radencich,
SCHOOL POWER, Free Spirit Publishing Inc. This page may be photocopied.

TITLE OF ASSIGNMENT: _____

_____

NUMBER OF PAGES: _____

General directions: Rate each of the FLIP categories on a 1-5 scale (5 = high, 1 = low). Circle your choice on the scale.

F **= FRIENDLINESS:** "How friendly is my reading assignment?"

Examine your assignment to see if it includes these friendly features. Give it a "5" if it includes most of them. Give it a "1" if it includes very few of them. Rate it somewhere in between if it has some of these friendly features.

Table of contents	Chapter introductions	Margin notes
Key terms highlighted	Pictures	Index
Headings	Study questions	Graphs
Signal words	Glossary	Subheadings
Chapter summary	Charts	List of key facts

1　　　**2**　　　**3**　　　**4**　　　**5**　　　**Friendliness rating:** _____

VERY UNFRIENDLY　　　　　　　　　　　VERY FRIENDLY

 = LANGUAGE: "How difficult is the language in my reading assignment?"

Choose three paragraphs from different parts of your assignment. Read each paragraph out loud. Give your assignment a "5" if the paragraphs have no new words and mostly comfortable sentences. Give it a "1" if they have many new words and mostly complicated sentences.

1　　　**2**　　　**3**　　　**4**　　　**5**　　　**Language rating:** _____

VERY EASY　　　　　　　　　　　VERY DIFFICULT

FLIP Chart used by permission of International Reading Association.
Copyright © 1992 by Jeanne Schumm and Marguerite Radencich,
SCHOOL POWER, Free Spirit Publishing Inc. This page may be photocopied.

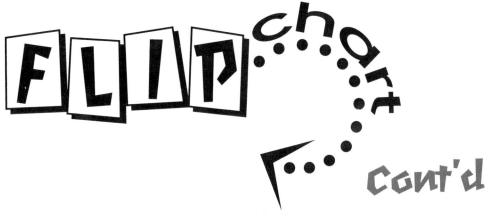

I = INTEREST: "How interesting is my reading assignment?"

Skim your assignment. Read the title, introduction, headings, subheadings, and summary. Look at the pictures and graphics. Give it a "5" if you can't wait to read the whole thing. Give it a "1" if it looks dull and boring to you—if you're really going to have to work to concentrate on it.

1   **2**   **3**   **4**   **5**   **Interest rating:** _____
_____
NOT INTERESTING   VERY INTERESTING

P = PRIOR KNOWLEDGE: "What do I already know about the material covered in my reading assignment?"

Think about the title, introduction, headings, subheadings, and summary. Give your assignment a "5" if it's old news to you. Give it a "1" if you've never even heard of the subject before now.

1   **2**   **3**   **4**   **5**   **Prior knowledge rating:** _____
_____
NOT FAMILIAR   VERY FAMILIAR

Scoring

Add up your ratings to find your overall rating: _____

Interpreting Your Score

17-20 rating points: The reading level should feel *comfortable* to you

12-16 rating points: The reading level should feel *somewhat comfortable* to you

4-11 rating points: The reading level may feel *uncomfortable* to you

FLIP Chart used by permission of International Reading Association.
Copyright © 1992 by Jeanne Schumm and Marguerite Radencich,
SCHOOL POWER, Free Spirit Publishing Inc. This page may be photocopied.

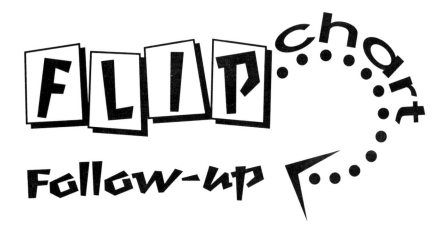

My purpose for reading is (circle one):

a. for personal pleasure

b. to prepare for class discussions

c. to answer written questions for class assignments or homework

d. to prepare for a test

e. other:

_____

My reading rate should be (circle one):

a. slow (allowing time for rereading if necessary)

b. medium (careful and analytical)

c. rapid (steady, skipping sections that contain information I already know)

My reading budget is:

Chunk #1, pages _____ - _____, estimated time _____ minutes

Chunk #2, pages _____ - _____, estimated time _____ minutes

Chunk #3, pages _____ - _____, estimated time _____ minutes

Chunk #4, pages _____ - _____, estimated time _____ minutes

Total Estimated Time: _____ minutes

FLIP Follow-up Chart used by permission of International Reading Association.
Copyright © 1992 by Jeanne Schumm and Marguerite Radencich,
SCHOOL POWER, Free Spirit Publishing Inc. This page may be photocopied.

Literature Study Guide

Title: _____

Author: _____

Type of story (mystery, historical fiction,
romance, etc.): _____

Setting

1. Time

Historical period _____

Duration (over what period of time does the story take place?

Examples: one day, several weeks, one hundred years)

_____

2. Place

Geographical location _____

Scenes (where does most of the story take place? Examples:

outdoors, in someone's home, in a magician's castle) _____

_____

Main Characters

1. Name _____

Physical description _____

_____

Personality description _____

_____

How does this character change during the story?

_____

_____

Copyright © 1992 by Jeanne Schumm and Marguerite Radencich,
SCHOOL POWER, Free Spirit Publishing Inc. This page may be photocopied.

Main Characters, cont'd

2. Name _____

Physical description _____

_____

Personality description _____

_____

How does this character change during the story?

_____

_____

3. Name _____

Physical description _____

_____

Personality description _____

_____

How does this character change during the story?

_____

_____

The problem of the story

_____

_____

_____

The plot (list 5 or 6 major events)

1. _____

2. _____

3. _____

4. _____

5. _____

6. _____

Copyright © 1992 by Jeanne Schumm and Marguerite Radencich,
SCHOOL POWER, Free Spirit Publishing Inc. This page may be photocopied.

How the problem was resolved

_____

_____

_____

_____

New or challenging vocabulary words

_____

_____

_____

_____

What will you remember most about this story?

_____

_____

_____

_____

Your opinion of this story

1. What you liked about it: _____

_____

_____

2. What you didn't like about it: _____

_____

_____

Would you recommend this story to a friend?

Yes ☐   No ☐

Copyright © 1992 by Jeanne Schumm and Marguerite Radencich,
SCHOOL POWER, Free Spirit Publishing Inc. This page may be photocopied.

A-OK check-list

Title: _____

Name of Author: _____

Name of Editor: _____

MOK (Meaning OK?)   Yes   No

"Does it make sense?"   ☐ ☐

"Is it concise and to the point?"   ☐ ☐

"Is it complete?"   ☐ ☐

"Does it say what I really want to say?"   ☐ ☐

"Are my facts correct?"   ☐ ☐

"Is there an introduction?"   ☐ ☐

"Is there a conclusion?"   ☐ ☐

POK (Paragraph OK?)

"Is it indented?"   ☐ ☐

"Is it made up of sentences related to ONE main idea?"   ☐ ☐

"Is it connected logically with paragraphs that come before or after?"   ☐ ☐

SOK (Sentence OK?)

"Does it start with a capital letter?"   ☐ ☐

"Does it end with the correct punctuation mark?"   ☐ ☐

Yes   No

"Is other punctuation used correctly?"   ☐ ☐

"Is it a complete sentence?"   ☐ ☐

"Does it express a complete thought?"   ☐ ☐

"Do the subject and verb agree?"

"Is its meaning clear?"

WOK (Word OK?)

"Is it spelled correctly?"   ☐ ☐

"Is it capitalized correctly?"   ☐ ☐

"Is it used correctly?"   ☐ ☐

"Is it over-used?"   ☐ ☐

"Is it slang?"   ☐ ☐

"Is it the VERY BEST word?"   ☐ ☐

NOK (Neatness OK?)

"Does it follow the required format?"   ☐ ☐

"Have I used my best handwriting?"   ☐ ☐

Adapted with permission of _Reading: Exploration and Discovery._
Copyright © 1992 by Jeanne Schumm and Marguerite Radencich,
SCHOOL POWER, Free Spirit Publishing Inc. This page may be photocopied.

101

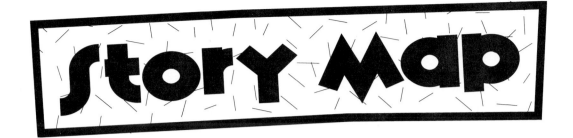

Story Map

SETTING

Time: _____

Place: _____

CHARACTERS

Name: _____

Description: _____

_____

_____

_____

_____

Name: _____

Description: _____

_____

_____

_____

_____

Name: _____

Description: _____

_____

_____

_____

_____

Copyright © 1992 by Jeanne Schumm and Marguerite Radencich,
SCHOOL POWER, Free Spirit Publishing Inc. This page may be photocopied.

STORY MAP Cont'd

EVENTS

1. _____
   _____
   _____
   _____

2. _____
   _____
   _____
   _____

3. _____
   _____
   _____

4. _____
   _____
   _____

5. _____
   _____
   _____
   _____

PROBLEMS

_____
_____
_____
_____
_____
_____
_____
_____
_____

SOLUTIONS

_____
_____
_____
_____
_____
_____
_____
_____
_____

104

Copyright © 1992 by Jeanne Schumm and Marguerite Radencich,
SCHOOL POWER, Free Spirit Publishing Inc. This page may be photocopied.

BOOK REPORT Fiction

I. INTRODUCTION

a. Title of book: _____

b. Author: _____

c. Type of book (example: mystery, adventure, fantasy): _____

d. Setting of book

Time: _____

Place: _____

e. Why I read this book: _____

_____

II. CHARACTERS

a. Main character (name and description):

_____

_____

_____

b. Other important characters (names and descriptions):

_____

_____

_____

_____

_____

_____

Copyright © 1992 by Jeanne Schumm and Marguerite Radencich,
SCHOOL POWER, Free Spirit Publishing Inc. This page may be photocopied.

Fiction Book cont'd

III. SUMMARY OF PLOT

_____

_____

_____

_____

_____

_____

_____

IV. CRITIQUE

a. The part I liked best was:

_____

_____

_____

b. The part I liked least was:

_____

_____

_____

c. This book was (check one)

☐ hard to read

☐ easy to read

☐ in between

d. I (check one)

☐ would

☐ would not

recommend this book to someone else because:

_____

_____

Copyright © 1992 by Jeanne Schumm and Marguerite Radencich,
SCHOOL POWER, Free Spirit Publishing Inc. This page may be photocopied.

BOOK REPORT Non-Fiction

I. INTRODUCTION

a. Title of book: _____

b. Author: _____

c. Subject of book: _____

d. Why I read this book: _____

_____

_____

_____

II. SUMMARY OF BOOK

_____

_____

_____

_____

_____

_____

_____

_____

_____

_____

Copyright © 1992 by Jeanne Schumm and Marguerite Radencich,
SCHOOL POWER, Free Spirit Publishing Inc. This page may be photocopied.

Non-Fiction Book cont'd

III. NEW AND INTERESTING FACTS I LEARNED FROM READING THIS BOOK

_____

_____

_____

_____

_____

IV. CRITIQUE

a. The part I liked best was:

_____

_____

b. The part I liked least was:

_____

_____

_____

c. This book was (check one)

☐ hard to read

☐ easy to read

☐ in between

d. I (check one)

☐ would

☐ would not

recommend this book to someone else because:

_____

_____

Copyright © 1992 by Jeanne Schumm and Marguerite Radencich,
SCHOOL POWER, Free Spirit Publishing Inc. This page may be photocopied.

I. INTRODUCTION

a. Title of book: _____

b. Author: _____

c. Subject of book: _____

d. Why I read this book:

_____

_____

_____

_____

II. SUMMARY OF BOOK

a. What I learned about the person's life: _____

_____

_____

_____

b. What I learned about the person's major achievements: _____

_____

_____

_____

_____

_____

Copyright © 1992 by Jeanne Schumm and Marguerite Radencich,
SCHOOL POWER, Free Spirit Publishing Inc. This page may be photocopied.

109

Biography Book cont'd

III. PROBLEMS

a. The major problem in the person's life was:

_____

_____

b. How this problem was solved:

_____

_____

IV. WHY THIS PERSON IS REMEMBERED OR ADMIRED TODAY

_____

_____

V. CRITIQUE

a. The part I liked best was:

_____

_____

_____

b. The part I liked least was:

_____

_____

_____

c. This book was (check one)

☐ hard to read

☐ easy to read

☐ in between

d. I (check one)

☐ would

☐ would not

recommend this book to someone else because:

_____

_____

Copyright © 1992 by Jeanne Schumm and Marguerite Radencich, SCHOOL POWER, Free Spirit Publishing Inc. This page may be photocopied.

RESEARCH PAPER Checklist

ASSIGNMENT: To write a term paper on _____

_____

_____

DUE DATE: _____

REQUIREMENTS:

My paper will need:

☐ title page

☐ table of contents

☐ bibliography

☐ graphics

What kinds of graphics? _____

It should be:

☐ typed

☐ doublespaced

☐ handwritten OK

STEPS: DATE DUE   DATE DONE

☐ **1.** Choose a topic.   _____   _____

☐ **2.** Write a thesis sentence. Have it approved by the teacher.   _____   _____

☐ **3.** Do library research.   _____   _____

SOURCES:

_____   _____   _____

_____   _____   _____

_____   _____   _____

☐ **4.** Contact community resources for information.   _____   _____

NAMES OF RESOURCES:

_____   _____   _____

_____   _____   _____

_____   _____   _____

Copyright © 1992 by Jeanne Schumm and Marguerite Radencich,
SCHOOL POWER, Free Spirit Publishing Inc. This page may be photocopied.

RESEARCH PAPER Checklist cont'd

☐ **5.** Write letters to request information from national sources.
WROTE LETTERS TO:

	DATE DUE	DATE DONE
_____	_____	_____
_____	_____	_____
_____	_____	_____
_____	_____	_____

☐ **6.** Take notes.
TOOK NOTES FROM THESE SOURCES:

_____	_____	_____
_____	_____	_____
_____	_____	_____
_____	_____	_____
_____	_____	_____
_____	_____	_____
_____	_____	_____

☐ **7.** Make a writing plan. _____ _____

☐ **8.** Write a rough draft. _____ _____

☐ **9.** Revise and edit rough draft; make corrections. _____ _____

☐ **10.** Write the final draft. _____ _____

☐ **11.** Turn the final draft in on time. _____ _____

Copyright © 1992 by Jeanne Schumm and Marguerite Radencich,
SCHOOL POWER, Free Spirit Publishing Inc. This page may be photocopied.

Spelling Demons

about
address
advise
again
all right
along
already
although
always
among
April
arithmetic
aunt
awhile

balloon
because
been
before
birthday
blue
bought
built
busy
buy

children
chocolate
choose
Christmas
close
color
come
coming
cough
could
couldn't
country
cousin
cupboard

dairy
dear
decorate

didn't
doctor
does

early
Easter
easy
enough
every
everybody

favorite
February
fierce
first
football
forty
fourth
Friday
friend
fuel

getting
goes
grade
guard
guess

half
Halloween
handkerchief
haven't
having
hear
heard
height
hello
here
hospital
hour
house

instead

knew
know

laid
latter
lessons
letter
little
loose
loving

making
many
maybe
minute
morning
mother

name
neither
nice
none

o'clock
off
often
once
outside

party
peace
people
piece
played
plays
please
poison
practice
pretty
principal

quarter
quit
quite

raise
read
ready
receive

received
remember
right
rough
route

said
Santa Claus
Saturday
says
school
schoolhouse
several
shoes
since
skiing
skis
some
something
sometime
soon
store
straight
studying
sugar
summer
Sunday
suppose
sure
surely
surprise
surrounded
swimming

teacher
tear
terrible
Thanksgiving
their
there
they
though
thought

through
tired
together
tomorrow
tonight
too
toys
train
traveling
trouble
truly
Tuesday
two

until
used

vacation
very

wear
weather
weigh
were
we're
when
where
which
white
whole
women
would
write
writing
wrote

you
your
you're

Copyright © 1992 by Jeanne Schumm and Marguerite Radencich, SCHOOL POWER, Free Spirit Publishing Inc. This page may be photocopied.

Spelling Demons reprinted with permission of Edward Fry, Ph.D.

Spelling Demons II

absence
acceptable
accommodate
accustom
ache
achievement
acquire
across
adolescent
advantageous
advertisement
advice
against
aisle
amateur
analyze
annually
anticipated
apparent
appreciate
arctic
arguing
argument
arrangement
athlete

bargain
belief
beneficial
benefited
breathe
Britain
bury
business

calendar
category
cemetery
certainly
cite
comparative
concede
conceive

condemn
conscience
conscientious
conscious
controversial
controversy
council
criticize

definitely
definition
descendant
describe
description
desert
dilemma
diligence
dining
disastrous
discipline
disease
dissatisfied

endeavor
effect
embarrass
emigrate
environment
especially
exaggerate
exceed
except
exercise
exhausted
existence
experience
explanation

fascinate
formerly

gaiety
gauge
grammar

guarantee
guidance

height
heroes
hypocrite

incredible
interest
interrupt
irrelevant
its

jealousy

led
leisurely
license
lieutenant
listener
lose
luxury

magnificent
maneuver
marriage
mathematics
medicine
mere
miniature
miscellaneous
mischief
moral
muscle
mysterious

necessary
niece
noticeable
numerous

occasion
occurred
occurrence
occurring

opinion
opportunity

paid
parallel
paralyzed
particular
performance
personal
personnel
pleasant
politician
portrayed
possession
possible
practical
preferred
prejudice
prepare
prescription
prestige
prevalent
principal
principle
privilege
probably
procedure
proceed
profession
professor
prominent
pursue

quiet

receipt
receive
recommend
referring
renowned
repetition
restaurant
rhythm

saucer
seize
sense
separate
sergeant
shining
similar
sincerely
sophomore
stationary
studying
substantial
subtle
succeed
succession
supersede
surprise
susceptible

technique
thorough
tragedy
transferred
tremendous

unnecessary

vacuum
valuable
vegetable
vengeance
villain
visible

waive
woman
wrench
write
writing

yacht

Copyright © 1992 by Jeanne Schumm and Marguerite Radencich, SCHOOL POWER, Free Spirit Publishing Inc. This page may be photocopied.

Spelling Demons II reprinted with permission of Edward Fry, Ph.D.

Record the number of minutes you spend on each study activity. Do this for one study session, or a week's worth. Find out how you're spending your study time. Decide if you need to make changes in your study habits.

Today's Date: _____

MINUTES SPENT	STUDY ACTIVITY
_____	Getting ready to study
_____	Completing my homework assignments
_____	Checking my homework assignments
_____	Identifying and quizzing myself on important facts and terms
_____	Previewing the chapter(s)
_____	Active reading (outlining, taking notes, semantic mapping, summarizing, annotating, highlighting, making flash cards)
_____	Comparing chapter notes with a friend
_____	Quizzing myself on chapter notes
_____	Rewriting and revising chapter notes
_____	Comparing class notes with a friend
_____	Highlighting class notes
_____	Quizzing myself on class notes
_____	Reading extra material for background
_____	Merging class notes and chapter notes
_____	Making up sample test questions
_____	Taping my sample questions and answers
_____	Listening to my study tape
_____	Getting study materials together to take to school
_____	_____
_____	_____
_____	_____

What do I need to spend MORE time doing? _____

_____

_____

What do I need to spend LESS time doing? _____

_____

_____

Copyright © 1992 by Jeanne Schumm and Marguerite Radencich,
SCHOOL POWER, Free Spirit Publishing Inc. This page may be photocopied.

About the Authors

Jeanne Shay Schumm, Ph.D., is Assistant Professor at the University of Miami in Coral Gables, Florida. She teaches graduate and undergraduate courses in reading and language arts instruction. Dr. Schumm is also the Director of the university's Student Literacy Corps, a program that trains university students to tutor in the public schools. She has published many research and practical articles and currently has a regular column in the *Journal of Reading*.

Marguerite C. Radencich, Ph.D., is a K-Adult Reading Supervisor for Dade County Public Schools, Miami, Florida, and an adjunct professor at several universities. She has taught at elementary and secondary school levels. She has published numerous professional articles and is coauthor with Dr. Gloria Knchinskas of *The Semantic Mapper* and *The Literary Mapper*, vocabulary development programs published by Teacher Support Software.

School Power! is the second book Jeanne and Margie have written for Free Spirit Publishing. Their first, *How to Help Your Child with Homework*, was published in 1988.

123

MORE FREE SPIRIT BOOKS

Making the Most of Today:
Daily Readings for Young People on Self-Awareness, Creativity, and Self-Esteem
by Pamela Espeland and Rosemary Wallner
Guides young people through a year of positive thinking, problem-solving, and practical lifeskills—the keys to making the most of every day.
$8.95; 392 pp; s/c; 4" × 7"; ISBN 0-915793-33-4

Stick Up for Yourself!
Every Kid's Guide to Personal Power and Positive Self-Esteem
by Gershen Kaufman, Ph.D., and Lev Raphael, Ph.D.
Readers find out that they are worth sticking up for, and learn to assert themselves in meaningful ways.
$8.95; 96 pp; s/c; illus.; 6" × 9"; ISBN 0-915793-17-2

Also Available:
A Teacher's Guide to Stick Up for Yourself
$14.95; 128 pp; s/c; 8 1/2" × 11"; ISBN 0-915793-31-8

Psychology for Kids:
40 Fun Tests That Help You Learn About Yourself
by Jonni Kincher
This book begins a journey of self-discovery that leads to greater personal freedom for a lifetime.
$14.95; 152 pp; illus.; 8 1/2" × 11"; ISBN 0-915793-85-7

It's All in Your Head: *A Guide to Understanding Your Brain and Boosting Your Brain Power,*
Revised and Updated Edition
by Susan L. Barrett
An "owner's manual" on the brain that includes information about intelligence and creativity, the difference between brain and mind, how we learn and remember, and more.
$9.95; 160 pp; s/c; illus.; 6" × 9"; ISBN 0-915793-45-8

Also Available:
A Teacher's Guide to It's All in Your Head
$6.95; 52 pp; s/c; 8 1/2" × 11"; ISBN 0-915793-46-6

The School Survival Guide for Kids with LD*
**(Learning Differences):* *Ways to Make Learning Easier and More Fun*
by Rhoda Cummings, Ed.D., and Gary Fisher, Ph.D.
Gives kids with LD specific tips and strategies for improving their skills in reading, writing, spelling, math, and more.
$10.95; 176 pp; s/c; illus.; 6" × 9"; ISBN 0-915793-32-6

Kidstories:
Biographies of 20 Young People You'd Like to Know
by Jim Delisle, Ph.D.
Learn from and enjoy real stories about real kids today. Includes discussion questions and resource listings.
$9.95; 176 pp; s/c; illus.; 6" × 9"; ISBN 0-915793-34-2

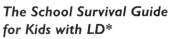

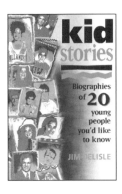

Find these books in your favorite bookstore, or write or call:

Free Spirit Publishing Inc.
400 First Avenue North, Suite 616
Minneapolis, MN 55401-1730
Toll-free (800) 735-7323, Local (612) 338-2068
Fax (612) 337-5050, E-mail help4kids@freespirit.com